# Not Your Mother's Book . . .
## On Family

Created and Edited by
Dahlynn McKowen,
Ken McKowen and Linda O'Connell

Published by
Publishing Syndicate

PO Box 607
Orangevale California 95662
www.PublishingSyndicate.com

# Not Your Mother's Book . . .
## On Family

*We would like to thank the many individuals
who granted us permission to reprint their stories.
See the complete listing beginning on page 288.*

Edited by Dahlynn McKowen,
Ken McKowen and Linda O'Connell
Cover and Book Design by Publishing Syndicate
Cover photo: Andresr/Shutterstock.com
Copyeditor: Dahlynn McKowen
Proofreader: Pat Nelson

Published by
**Publishing Syndicate**
PO Box 607
Orangevale California 95662

www.PublishingSyndicate.com
www.Facebook.com/PublishingSyndicate
Twitter: @PublishingSynd

Print Edition ISBN: 978-1-938778-16-2
EPUB Digital Edition ISBN: 978-1-938778-17-9
MOBI Digital Edition ISBN 978-938778-30-8
Library of Congress Control Number 2013907707

Printed in Canada.

This book is a collaborative effort. Writers from all over the world submitted their work for consideration, with 60 stories making the final cut. All contributors are compensated for their stories.

Publishing Syndicate strongly encourages you to submit your story for one of its many anthologies.

**For information on how to submit your story, see page 296 or go to www.PublishingSyndicate.com.**

# Dedication

## This book is dedicated to the families of our contributors

May these stories remind you of your early years, when someone always sang your praises or wiped away your tears.

May these stories call to mind your own family's mischief makers, especially if you were one of the "disturbers."

May these stories stir up memories of meals your family shared, the aromas in your kitchen, the food lovingly prepared.

May these stories transport you back to those trips you thought would never end, when claims were staked on window seats and adventure lay 'round every bend.

May these stories open up your listening ears, help you recall your elders' voices, words of wisdom, observations, and some stories you thought you'd never hear.

May these stories inspire you to make up games, bend rules, take turns and chances, as you engage in your own family fun. You are never too old to play.

May these stories help you realize that every family has "Oh, crap!" moments. Keep in mind, you have the right to remain silent . . . or write your own version.

*~~ Linda O'Connell*

# CONTENTS

# 7 You Just Never Know

# 8 All in the Family

# Acknowledgments

**From Linda:**

Thank you to my supportive, humorous and computer-savvy husband, Bill. He is my champion.

Thank you to Dianna Graveman, co-creator of *Not Your Mother's Book . . . On Being a Mom*. Dianna talked me up and she talked me down when I had frustrating computer issues, many a result of operator error.

And thank you to my blended and extended family for providing me with many "laugh lines" and bringing immense pride and joy to my life.

**From Dahlynn and Ken:**

Thanks to Dahlynn's teen son Shawn. Hooray! Another book is out the door and life at home can return to normal, until the next book.

Thank you to Shayla Seay. You keep us on the straight and narrow and also keep our filing system—both hard copy and online—updated and organized, all at the same time.

A big thanks to Terri Elders for reading the galleys for us. Your keen eye is always welcomed and appreciated!

And thank you to Pat Nelson for proofing another book. We learn something new every time we go through this process with you. When it comes to "style," you are the man . . . er, woman.

**And from all of us at Publishing Syndicate:**

A special thanks to the many writers who submitted stories for this book. Without you, this book would not have come together like it did. Your stories were wonderful and we thank you for sharing them with us and the world. We only wish we could have printed every story submitted.

Keep those stories coming in for future NYMB titles: www.PublishingSyndicate.com.

# Introduction

*"Happiness is having a large, loving, caring,
close-knit family ... in another city."*
~~ George Burns

*"Having a family is like having
a bowling alley installed in your brain."*
~~ Martin Mull

The word "family" has different connotations for each of us. The word may conjure early memories of a father's hug, a mother's kiss, a hand to hold, a shoulder to cry on or an ear to listen to your worst fears, highest hopes and earliest dreams.

Whether you consider your family typical, ideal, normal or dysfunctional, every member has at least one thing in common—a shared bond, not just a lineage. No matter how you are connected—either by genetics or association—your nuclear, blended or extended family represents a unique thread woven into a tapestry of personalities: nutty, nice, silly, sensible and everything in between.

Granted, your opinions of one another may change day-to-day, drama-to-drama. Your family's communication style may be bantering and boisterous or polite, calm and in control. Some families shout to be heard, while others have mastered the art of non-verbal communication. Surely, you have been praised with a smile or reprimanded with an expression. Even toddlers recognize "the look" and teens are quick to react to it, that is, when they're not giving it.

About those two quotes at the beginning of the introduction, it was hard to choose which one to use. Comic genius George Burns was born in 1896 and passed away 100 years later, while Martin Mull, an accomplished American actor, was born in 1943 and still graces our TV and movie screens today. Both men are fathers, and both have used the theme of family in their work. What is interesting is that the two men—born in different generations—share the same perspective when it comes to the reality of family.

While you can't choose your family, you have the power to choose how to be part of a family. No one can take that away from you. So when Grandpa absent-mindedly tells you the same story for the zillionth time, or your sister shares your deepest, darkest secret on Facebook, you can choose to either go crazy or grant forgiveness. Because they are your loving, crazy, zany family . . . and you can't help but love them. Or as George says, you can move to another city!

~~ *Linda O'Connell*

# CHAPTER ONE

# The Early Years

It's only cute because they're little.

# A Word Repeated

by
Lisa Ricard Claro

At three years old, my son, Joey, like most children that age, displayed the tendencies of a mynah bird. A word heard became a word repeated. Because of this, my husband, Joe, and I did our level best to keep our vocabulary squeaky clean.

But despite our best efforts, the occasional swear word made its way past our lips and into the ears of our son, who, of course, repeated it. Being the smart tyke that he was, his usage, though inappropriate due to his age, was often quite applicable to the circumstance. For instance:

When he tripped and fell down at the park: "Shit!"

When his building-block tower tumbled: "Shit!"

When his scoop of orange sherbet rolled off the cone and onto the ground: "Shit!"

Hearing that word come from his sweet little mouth had the effect of fingernails scraping on a chalkboard. Joe and I winced with every utterance. Of course, the fact that all other adults within earshot laughed their butts off was not lost on Joey, who considered this to be encouragement to continue the practice, despite our parental reprimands.

After a few embarrassing outbursts, Joe and I sat our little smarty-pants down and explained that there are some words adults can say that children cannot. We suggested other words would be more appropriate for him, and he learned in no uncertain terms that "shit" could, and had better, be replaced with the likes of "sugar," "darn" or "fudge."

Joey grasped those words well and we left the S-word and all its embarrassment behind us. In an effort to prevent further verbal no-no's, Joe and I cleaned up our act, being more careful than ever to keep our vocabulary Joey-appropriate. We had some slips, the expected, "Oh, shii-ugar!" and "Shii-darn!" But for the most part, our perseverance resulted in success, and our little family enjoyed a mostly expletive-free environment.

And so it was that one night the Claro family found itself on an airplane winging its way to Chicago. The flight was full, a 747 packed with people, most of whom had, no doubt, cringed during the embarkation process when Joe and I climbed aboard with a backpack full of toys and an active, curious toddler in tow.

The year was 1985. Back then, a child was not required to claim his or her own seat during air travel—a parent's lap was deemed an acceptable spot for little ones in flight. Therefore, Joe and I traded Joey back and forth between us as necessary, mindful of the comfort of our fellow passengers. I occupied the window seat, Joe sat in the center seat and a pleasant gentleman occupied the aisle seat. Eager to keep our little angel from being a nuisance, Joe and I kept Joey busy with stories and coloring books and other toys, and occasionally bribed his silence with snacks and juice drinks.

Joey proved himself a perfect traveler throughout the three-and-a-half-hour flight. He played quietly, alternating between his daddy and me, and otherwise comported himself as a well-behaved little gentleman. The flight could not have gone more smoothly, and my husband and I beamed with pride at our son's excellent behavior.

Between the hours of 10 and 11 P.M., activity on the plane quieted. The cabin lights were dimmed, and though some passengers read books or magazines, most took the opportunity to doze.

Joey grew restless and stood up, planting his sneakered feet on his daddy's thighs. Joe held him around the waist, and Joey grabbed the seatback in front of him for added steadiness. He lifted to his tippy-toes and peered over the seat, surveying the sea of heads and bodies in front of him, twisting about to see those behind. The cabin was dim and quiet, with only an occasional cough to pierce the hum of the engines.

And then it happened.

"Say darn or sugar, but never say SHIT!"

Three pregnant seconds of silence followed Joey's boisterous proclamation to all. And then the entire plane of passengers erupted with laughter. The man in the seat beside Joe literally guffawed himself to tears.

Joe sat with his hands on Joey's waist, eyes wide. We exchanged surprised and embarrassed glances. I bit my lip and shrank down into my seat, but Joe had nowhere to hide as everybody craned their necks to catch a look at the cute little guy who had made the enthusiastic announcement. And Joey, thrilled and encouraged by the hilarious response, bounced on his toes and repeated his directive with unabashed glee.

I'm here to tell you that no matter how pointed the explanation, no matter the words of choice, there is no way to convince a humor-inclined three-year-old that such an obviously funny phrase is bad. How can it be bad when everyone who hears it laughs?

For weeks, Joe and I ventured forth tentatively, wondering when and if another embarrassing outburst might occur, and hoping our little guy would forget about making grown-ups laugh.

One day, heading into the grocery store, I looked heavenward and begged for the darn/sugar/shit phrase to be abolished. *Surely*, I prayed, *there must be an end to this. Can't he find something else to say?*

As I headed into the busy produce department with a cheerful Joey seated in the grocery cart, I learned to be careful what I asked for. My little boy made the following announcement at the top of his lungs: "Bert and Ernie are boys. That means they have a PENIS!"

Well, at least he didn't say, "Shit!"

Joey

# Are You Game?

by
Cathi LaMarche

"It must've been wonderful growing up with an older brother to protect you," my friend mentioned over coffee.

"Hmm . . . you have sisters, don't you?" I asked. I sipped my latte and imagined a gentler childhood, playing dress-up and tea party, complete with decorative invitations and tiaras. Instead, I had suffered enemy invasions by G.I. Joes with firecrackers strapped to their backs, threatening to take my Barbies and me hostage. "Brothers are rough. Loud. Noisome," I offered.

She laughed. "But they keep an eye on their younger sisters. I didn't have that luxury."

Luxury? Summoning passersby to rescue me from the latest game of "I'm going to slug your arm until it goes numb" or "I'll pin you down and break wind in your face" was not my idea of a privileged childhood.

When I was 11, my brother Mike pointed to the parka

with the foot-long snorkel jutting out and said, "Hey, put this on for a minute."

Even though the outside temperature had climbed to 80 degrees by noon, I shrugged and donned the down-filled coat. Zipping it, I stopped short of pulling the snorkel over my head, but Mike was kind enough to do it for me. And he continued zipping. And zipping. And zipping.

"Oh, crap," he said, holding the pull-tab in his hand.

A drop of sweat, or 10, trickled down my back. "Um, you can still unzip me, right?"

Mike grabbed the snorkel and tried to pry the zipper open, to no avail. "Not sure."

My face reddened as I started to cry, and the air moistened within the narrow tunnel that had swallowed my head. "Call Mom or Dad!" I bellowed through my fleece-lined megaphone. "It's too hot in here. I can't breathe. I'm going to die!"

Mike sighed. "You're not going to die. Besides, Mom and Dad are at work. They'll kill us for making them come home."

"You mean they'll kill you."

"Whatever. I'll figure something out." Mike grabbed a pair of needle-nose pliers from the toolbox. After failing to free me, he shrugged. "In less than five hours, Dad will be home."

I screamed. I cried. I begged. All of which made me hotter.

"What's for lunch?" Mike asked, glancing at me. "Oh, sorry. I suppose you can't eat with that snorkel sticking out like that."

Perhaps it was the way I stood in front of the open freezer, funneling cold air down the snorkel, or the way I positioned myself by the oscillating fan and whimpered like an injured animal, but Mike eventually fed me ice cream with a long sundae spoon. Two bowls of chocolate-chocolate chip and all had been forgiven.

A few weeks later, Mike pointed to an area rug on the basement floor. "Hey, why don't you lie down on the edge of the rug?"

"Why?" I asked.

"It's a cool game called . . . uh, 'bug in a rug.'"

I hesitated.

"Where did you learn it?"

"A friend's house. Everyone's playing it."

I stared at the rug.

"Fine. If you don't want to play, I'll find someone else." Mike turned to leave. "Your loss."

"No." I blocked his path. "I'll play." I went to the edge of the rug and eased myself down.

"Put your arms at your sides, like a soldier."

I dropped my arms and waited for the rest of the rules. "Now what?"

He quickly rolled me up like a taquito and left the premises, leaving me to shimmy, rock and squirm my way to freedom.

On a rainy Saturday, he placed giant, glow-in-the-dark super balls under the living room table lamp and flipped the light on. Lord knows how many pieces of bubblegum Mike had to buy to get them. He juiced the balls up under the light all day until they radiated neon green.

"What are those for?" I asked, passing through the room.

He smiled. "Are you game?"

"Maybe."

"It's called 'super-ball war.'" He motioned me into the basement, and I turned on the light.

"No. We need to keep the lights off. They're glow-in-the dark, remember?"

I flipped off the light and waited for his instructions.

"Now, you're going to stand there, and I'm going to throw the balls at you."

"You mean 'to me'?"

"Yeah. Sure. Then it will be your turn to throw them back."

The basement was pitch-black, and the balls were suspended in the air as he stockpiled the ammo in his hand.

Soon, "ouch!" and "yeow!" echoed off the cinder-block walls as he pelted me with the lighted projectiles. He laughed each time I cried out, and his feet shuffled across the floor to snag the balls for another round of pummeling.

After a ball pelted my cheek so hard that it left an immediate welt, I said, "It's not funny." I quickly decided it was my turn to impart some suffering onto Mike, so I darted toward one of the glowing spheres.

As did he.

Thunk! We knocked noggins. My lip split and warm blood trickled down my chin.

"Why'd you go and do that?" Mike said as he flipped on the light. He plucked the balls from the floor and announced, "Game over," as he rubbed his forehead.

The teenage years brought more dangerous games that included BB guns, minibikes and matches, threatening to end my life before I hit high school. But miraculously, I survived.

As I stirred my coffee and peeled back the foil from my lemon poppy-seed muffin, my friend recalled her childhood memories of baking brownies in an Easy-Bake Oven and creating Jewel Magic masterpieces with her sisters on lazy Sunday afternoons. Mike would've concocted a game of "how long can you hold your hand in the hot oven without flinching?" or "why put jewelry on a string when you can Krazy Glue it on your body?"

It was then I realized her stories lacked a sense of energy. Passion. Danger. I thought back again to our childhood games that seemed like torture at the time, and I smiled. The pain has faded. The stitches have been removed. A scar or two has remained.

Cool.

Cathi and Mike,
Christmas 1967

Cathi and Mike,
Christmas 1969

# Battle Strategies

by
Barbara Carpenter

When we were children, one of my younger brother's prized possessions was a genuine Hopalong Cassidy pocket-knife, complete with a textured plastic handle. A silver-colored image of the beloved cowboy astride his rearing horse was glued to the plastic. Billy managed to hold on to the knife for several months after the Christmas he received it. Unfortunately, the following summer he lost it in the park beside our house. He was only nine, but he stoically took his scolding from our parents for being careless with his possessions.

One Sunday afternoon, our little sister, five-year-old Bonnie, who was determined to learn how to play "jacks," had somehow coerced Billy into playing the game with her on the wide step at the front of our house. A boy about a year older and a lot bigger than Billy stopped his bicycle on the sidewalk and called to my brother.

"Hey, I just found a knife in the park."

"I bet it's mine," Billy announced. He left Bonnie on the step and walked over to the boy, who stood on the sidewalk. He had his bicycle balanced between his legs.

"How do you know it's yours?" he demanded.

"Because I lost mine over there," Billy gestured toward the park. Bonnie joined her brother. She looked from one to the other as the conversation progressed. From the living room window, my mother, dad and I could hear the discussion quite well. Dad got up from the couch and stood beside the window, where he could watch the situation unfold.

"That doesn't mean it's your knife," the boy stated. "It could be anybody's. When did you lose yours?"

"This summer. It's been a while—sometime after school was out," Billy said, nonchalantly putting his hands into his pockets. He was a negotiator. Bonnie, on the other hand, was a combatant. Both of them usually worked out confrontations to their own advantage, but her approach was more direct and much quicker. Only her age and size kept her from being the neighborhood avenger—or terror.

"Janie, come watch this," Dad said to my mother with a smile. Mom and I joined Dad at the window.

"Oh, yeah?" the boy challenged. "What did your knife look like?"

"It's a Hopalong Cassidy knife with a silver picture on the side."

The boy looked at the sidewalk and shifted his bicycle. "That don't mean nothin'," he countered. "What color is the handle?"

"Black. It has little ridges in it." Billy sounded calm.

His adversary kept one hand on the handlebar of his bike and withdrew the knife in question from his pocket. It was a Hopalong Cassidy knife.

"That's my knife," Billy told him.

"You can't prove it," the boy taunted. "You can't prove it's yours, and I'm gonna keep it." He started to put the knife back into his pocket.

Bonnie flew at the bigger boy with the fury of the just. "You give my brother back his knife!" she yelled, attacking him with both hands and pushing him, nearly toppling him to the sidewalk. He dropped the knife and it clattered onto the pavement. Totally unprepared for the attack, the boy grabbed the bike's handlebars with both hands to keep from falling.

Bonnie didn't let up. She continued to pummel the poor kid, using both fists, alternating them—*bam! bam! bam!*—which probably felt like ball-peen hammers. Billy ignored his sister's tirade and picked up the knife.

"Keep the old knife!" the boy shouted. With one last kick at the boy's bare shin, five-year-old Bonnie backed away. He found his balance and pedaled down the street, not looking back once.

"It's broke," Billy said.

Bonnie stared at the knife in his hand, and then looked up at her big brother's face. She put her hands on her hips, stepped away from him and glared after the enemy, who was already half a block away. "The silver piece came off when he dropped it, and the blade is all rusty," Billy continued.

"Maybe Daddy can fix it," Bonnie suggested.

Daddy, in the meantime, could not suppress his glee. Hot-tempered himself, his pride in this youngest offspring was justified. "Just look at that," he crowed.

"Well, there's no doubt whose daughter she is!" Mom muttered. "Can you try not to look so happy that she's just like you?"

By the time Billy and Bonnie came inside, Dad had himself a bit under control, while Mom and I pretended that we had not witnessed the altercation. Still unable to wipe the grin from his face, Dad examined the damaged knife. He led the way to his tool shop in the garage, where he restored the silver Hopalong Cassidy logo to its rightful place.

To this day, some 60 years later, Bonnie never fails to come rampaging to the rescue when any of her family is in trouble. On the other hand, Billy—the calm one—surveys any given situation and would still rather negotiate.

Barbara, age 11,
Billy, age 9
and Bonnie, age 5

# The Bathroom Mystery

by
Cathy C. Hall

Let me start with this qualifier: By the age of two or so, all of my kids were properly potty-trained. Unfortunately, this did not mean that all of my kids practiced good potty etiquette. Still, I was shocked when I walked into my downstairs guest bathroom, the one with the new wallpaper, and found brown lines streaking down the wall.

I'm pretty sure I screamed.

First, my husband came running.

"You are not going to believe this," I said, pointing to the stained and smelly wall.

"Well, don't look at me," he said.

Of course, I didn't think my husband was the guilty party. In fact, I was certain I knew exactly which kid was the guilty party. But I rounded up the usual suspects, just to give the appearance of being fair. Plus, I like to give guilty parties a chance to come clean, no pun intended.

Joey, Lane and John lined up in the family room, eyes wide. They recognized the look on Mommy's face.

"Somebody," I said, "used the downstairs bathroom. But he or she, for reasons I cannot begin to understand, chose not to use the toilet paper when he or she wiped."

Three sets of eyes grew wider.

"Somebody," I said, keying in on the wide eyes of my youngest, John, "decided to use his or her hand. And then wiped that hand on my NEW WALLPAPER!"

"Ewww," said Joey, the oldest. "It wasn't me."

My daughter, absolutely petrified and also completely grossed out, shook her head vigorously. That left John. The sweet, innocent baby of the family, who stared up at me, smiling.

"John," I said. "Do you know who did this?"

Of course we all knew who did this. To be honest, his hands gave him away. But we waited patiently for John to do the right thing and tell the truth.

"John? Who did this?" I asked again.

"It was the white dog," he said.

The week before, I'd come downstairs to find my neighbor's very large, white dog in my family room. I think I might have screamed then, too. We'd discussed the dog several times during the week. How had the dog ended up in our house? Had the dog come over here on his own and pushed open the kitchen door? Or had some kid—and we'd wondered if it hadn't been the kid who wanted a dog—"helped" the dog get into the house. Frankly, we suspected dog-loving John, but we'd never quite solved this mystery. So, you can imagine my surprise when John claimed the white dog had reappeared in our home, desperate to use the downstairs bathroom.

Still hopeful that he'd 'fess up, I said to John, "Those aren't paw prints on the wallpaper."

He just looked at me. I truly believe the child thought I'd buy the white dog story. But then I couldn't hold it a minute longer. John's sweet little face, the other kids' terrified faces, the WHITE DOG. I laughed aloud.

And then my husband laughed. The kids keeled over laughing, and in between all that laughter, we kept saying, "The white dog did it."

All those young'uns aren't so young anymore. But my grown-up kids still end up at my house frequently. And when they are, a mystery usually follows. Like, "Who left the soft drink out and didn't put the top back on?" Or, "Who left the wet towel on the floor?" Or, "Does anybody know where this stain on the carpet came from?"

Bet you can guess what they always say. "The white dog did it." And even after all these years, we still laugh. Because the family that laughs together, loves together.

But only a mom will clean poop off a bathroom wall.

John, now grown up, with chocolate pudding on his face. He claims the white dog did it!

# Head Over Heels

by
Mona Dawson

When I was 16 years old and in high school, I was only allowed to go out Friday or Saturday night, but not both. However, if I was with my big brother, who was two years older, I could pretty much do as he did because my parents felt secure that he'd watch over me. Knowing I would be safe, all my dad would say was not to stay out late. Not knowing what "late" meant since my brother had no curfew, I assumed I could do as he did. But I never pushed it. It was 1965 and democracy did not reign inside our family home.

At the time, I had a rare blood disease, which had not yet been diagnosed. I bruised and bled very easily, so my family was used to seeing me in some sort of messy state. Plus, being an only girl in a house with all boys, my parents—mostly, my father—were very protective of me.

One Friday night during my junior year of high school, I wanted to tag along with my big brother and one of his friends.

It was not uncommon for my friends and his to do things together. But this time he said I couldn't. However, after much pleading, whining and giving him my best puppy dog looks, he gave in. What a softie.

We drove around a while, ending up in Berkeley, the hippie capital of the world for me. At the time, we hadn't yet decided if we were hippies. Dad would never allow any part of that, so we were "flower children."

We ended up at the Claremont Hotel Club & Spa, a very old, huge, fancy place, much like the Del Coronado in San Diego. Opened in 1915, the hotel is set back into the Berkeley hills and is surrounded by an upscale neighborhood.

It was dark when we arrived, and my brother parked on a side street behind the hotel. As we crept through a backside parking lot, he urged both of us to be very quiet. At the end of the lot, we came to the rear of the building and looked up at the tall and elegant historical structure. The Claremont is a beautiful sight all lit up at night—the white building glows and because it sits high in the hills, it can be seen from many places throughout the San Francisco Bay Area.

We paused when we saw windows open in the basement area, which turned out to be the hotel's kitchen. One of the kitchen workers was standing outside, leaning on an open door and smoking. We waited in the shadows until he went back inside.

"What are we going to do here?" I asked.

My brother ignored my question and instead told me to stay right where I was, that he and his friend would be back in a minute. I stood there and watched them for a while until they were almost out of sight. I wore a black turtleneck sweater, a navy-and-green plaid A-line skirt that came to just above the knee, white socks and black tennis shoes. My hippy hair, still damp from my shower, hung long and straight down my back to my waist. I was a little nervous and began to feel cold. He was kidding himself if he thought I'd stay put alone in the dark behind this huge property.

So when they turned a corner at one edge of the building and were out of sight, I followed. As I turned the corner, I realized I'd have to soldier-crawl in order to get past the ground-level kitchen windows to avoid being seen by the dishwashers. I got down and scooted past the windows, hearing all the kitchen noises, praying I wouldn't get caught out there alone.

Once I passed the windows, I had to turn another corner. When I did, I saw my brother's friend go into a cylinder-shaped metal tube that ran up the side of the building to the top floor, the seventh. There was a shorter tube next to it which ran up the other side five stories high. My brother and his friend were inside the tallest one and I could hear them whispering something to each other.

When I reached the opening, I heard their muffled voices guiding each other as they climbed. I stepped inside. My face smacked into what appeared to be a metal wall. I couldn't tell because it was so dark. Using my hands on the sides of the tunnel and my tennis shoes for a good grip on the far side, I started to climb backward, scooting upward while listening to their instructions to each other. I realized I was climbing up in a circle. I paused at each floor level where there was an old barricaded door and a ledge just big enough to sit on.

"Did you hear that noise?" my brother asked his friend.

I stopped and stayed quiet, although my heart was pounding and I was breathing hard.

When they agreed there was no noise, they continued their climb. Then I heard my brother whisper that he'd reached the seventh floor and his friend said he was right behind. It was then I realized that this was the hotel's old fire escape, and they were going to slide down and probably right on top of me!

I bumped my head again and said, "Ouch!" a little too loudly.

My brother whispered "Mo, is that you?"

"Yes."

"Get down, now! You're going to get hurt," he said in a quiet but panicked voice.

"I want to slide, too," I whispered.

"Then stop where you are and slide from there," he whispered back. "How far up are you?"

"I'm almost to the fifth floor, but I want to slide down with you."

His friend agreed with my brother's advice. "You'd better listen. This is too dangerous."

I obeyed and climbed to the entrance to the fifth floor. My brother guided me with a whisper. "Turn around slowly and sit on the ledge at the entrance to the floor you're on. Then before you slide, lift your feet and take your hands off the sides of the tube. But DO NOT let your tennis shoes touch the slide."

He was still whispering, but I could tell he was very upset with me. But I didn't hear his last remark about my tennis shoes. Someone on the fifth floor heard our whispers and was questioning where the voices were coming from. So I let go of the sides. I didn't lift my feet and my tennis shoes stuck to the metal. I tumbled head over heels down five stories in a dark, dirty and extremely rusty cylinder.

*BAH BOOM! BAH BOOM! BAH BOOM!*

I rolled helplessly, floor after floor. The whole slide shook, and the rumbling was as horrific inside the hotel as inside the slide. It was the loudest thunder I'd ever heard. And it felt as though the cylinder would pull away from the building and come crashing down, bringing all three of us with it.

I came flying out of the opening of the tube as if I had been shot from a cannon. I slid face-first into the gravel at the tube's opening and several feet into the parking lot.

"What was that?!" my brother yelled.

"I think your sister fell down the slide!" his friend screamed.

"Mo! Are you OK? Talk to me," he groaned.

"I'm fine" I replied, scared and shaken.

"Don't move! We're coming down!" His tone told me he was really mad.

Since they were already at the seventh floor entrance to the old slide, I could hear the rush of air coming from inside the tube as they slid down: *Whoosh! Whoosh! Whoosh!* And their speed was picking up faster and faster. At the bottom, they flew out like rockets and landed in the gravel just past where I lay, except they landed on their butts, not their faces.

As I came back to my senses, one thought hit me: *Holy moly! I just fell five stories down the Claremont Hotel's antique fire escape and lived!* Then a second thought came, this one terrifying: *My parents are going to kill me!*

I slowly began to pull myself together, but my foot hurt and I couldn't stand. When I looked at my feet, both shoes were gone. So were my plaid A-line skirt, my black turtleneck and one sock. I wore only my slip and one sock and I was covered with rust and blood from head to toe. I was a red mess.

My brother's friend gave me his jacket as they looked at me with horror. Then they both grabbed me and ran to the car, carrying me the whole way. We heard the security guards exiting the building, running toward the slide area.

"I want to go home," I whimpered.

"Idiot!" he screamed at me, freaked out that our parents were going to kill us both.

"What were you thinking and how are you going to get into the house without Dad and Mom seeing you this way?"

I didn't care. I hurt everywhere and all I wanted was my bed. Forget cleaning up, forget the blood—I just wanted to hide in my bed.

I fell asleep on the way home, but soon was awakened by laughter.

"Man! I would have loved to have seen your sister come flying out like that."

"Didn't you hear her coming behind you?" my brother mildly scolded his buddy.

"No. I was so scared to be there in the first place. All I heard was your steps and mine."

"We should have stopped and looked for her clothes," my brother said.

"Are you kidding? Didn't you see security come around the corner after us? We just made it to the car in time."

Once at home, my brother went in the house through the back door to distract our parents and I crept quietly to my room. When they asked where I was, he said, "I think she might have gone to the bathroom. She'll be out in a minute."

But I didn't come out. I went into the bathroom, stressed, scared, hurt, bleeding and stained with rust. I looked in horror at my reflection in the mirror. My nose was bleeding, my cheek was bruised, my hands and knees were scraped and my hair was caked with everything red. Quickly, I showered and slipped into bed, falling sound asleep within seconds.

I got up early the next morning and tried to make myself look presentable. I covered the bruise on my cheek with make-up. Scratches and bruises were everywhere else on my body, so I wore long sleeves and jeans. I gingerly walked to the table for breakfast, every part of me screaming in pain. At least nothing was broken—just bruised—and, amazingly, I was alive. Smiling, as was her normal way, Mom asked me if I'd had fun with my brother since we'd come in much earlier than she'd expected.

"Yeah, hanging out with him is fun, but it wears me out."

I missed that plaid skirt for years to come and always thought of it fondly, with a secret smile on my face.

# On the Defensive

by
Paul Kent

I hereby volunteer my children for America's next major military operation. (Note to Defense Department: My three kids are highly skilled in D&D—disruption and destruction. If that's not an official military designation, it should be.)

Got a bridge that needs to come down? I've got a four-year-old for that. For bigger jobs—say, taking out an entire base complex—I'd recommend my older son. Need to crash a communications grid? Heck, my daughter could handle that.

OK, so I'm exaggerating just a bit. My youngest isn't actually four yet. But it's no stretch to say that all three of them are experts at smudging, marring, breaking, destroying and otherwise obliterating stuff—toys, games, books, DVDs, electronics, furniture, shrubs, you name it. Nothing withstands the blitzkrieg of the youth division.

Back before I had a family—when I knew much more about parenting—I told myself that physical possessions were secondary. Since the children came first, damage around the house wouldn't bother me.

I lied.

Actually, that wasn't so much deceit as it was ignorance. Yes, the kids are primary. Yes, the stuff is secondary. But who knew how much "secondary" the "primary" could thrash? Nearly everything our family owns is broken.

Perhaps this is all some kind of cosmic justice. From a distance of more than 35 years, I can still recall Mom's plaintive words after my brother and I shattered a favorite vase: "Why can't I have anything nice?"

Maybe she and I should start a club. Or maybe we should wield a club—to protect our stuff from the kids. What foul demon urges three-year-old Little Guy to use a Sharpie marker on Sweet Pea's dresser, sheets and bedroom door? Probably the same foul demon that caused Sweet Pea, at age three, to mark up another room in the house. Where does Bubba get the Hulk-like strength to ruin not one, but several door handles by the time he's seven? And why do all three kids like to jump up and down on the living room sofa? Well, actually, I do understand that . . . there's that cosmic justice thing, again.

Some of the destruction is ridiculously minor, but still maddening. Somehow, the thin metal rod on a very educational model-rocket launcher was snapped in half after someone jammed an equally educational music stand onto the launch pad. Was this some kind of "Music Appreciation for Space Aliens" program or just the typical squirrels-on-speed behavior of my three kids?

In the case of the musical launcher, which sounds a lot

like a Hardy Boys mystery, I want to believe there was some kind of playful imagination at work. It certainly got *my* imagination going—daydreams of how much money I'd have if I didn't need to repair, replace or otherwise revisit so much of the stuff around our home.

The kids' destructive ways were pushing me to the outer limits of patience when, backing my car from the garage one morning, I edged too close to the door and ripped off a side mirror. Because my kids are within eyesight of the computer screen at this very moment; my thoughts when I hit the door were not pretty.

That darned cosmic justice was working overtime, offering the not-so-gentle reminder that I, even I, am not perfect. I can accidentally break things and I am quick to seek others to blame. Though, in this particular case, I couldn't find a single underage scapegoat to blame for the minor accident. Rats!

So maybe it's time for a little grace. They are, after all, only kids. My kids. My family.

(Note to Defense Department: I'll touch base again in about 10 years.)

Paul with the kids, (l to r) Little Guy, Bubba and Sweet Pea

# Bunny Love

by
Tori Nichols

No parent wants to wake up to the terrifying sound of a child's screams. As my feet thundered down the hall to our girls' room, the sound of my heart beating in my ears nearly matched the intensity of the wailing.

My husband beat me there and flipped on the bedroom light. Sitting up in bed was our 11-year-old, mouth wide open, screaming like an actress in a horror film.

"It's OK, calm down. It's OK," I reassured Lori.

But was it?

What seemed to be sewage in radiating smears decorated Lori's half of the narrow, shared room. Deciphering the scene, my nurse's brain made a STAT assessment and came to the mistaken conclusion that my daughter's bowel had exploded. Her twin bed, nestled against the wall, was most assuredly ground zero of some event. The area looked like a war zone of paintball-style brown sludge. Lori's face was covered in a mud mask of the offending material and her yellow hair, standing on end in all directions, was streaked with a profusion of brown highlights.

I stepped forward, inspecting a glop of goop that was sliding down Lori's eyelid. Scooping it onto my finger revealed clues—the texture was creamy, but sticky. I took a cautious whiff. With raised eyebrows and the courage that only mothers have, I placed it on the tip of my tongue. My husband winced and held his breath. After a dramatic pause, I declared, "It's chocolate!"

Often, little girls are darlings of delight, lambs of love, angels to be adored. This tends to lure parents into the dream of an easy journey. Fair warning—sometimes this dream is interrupted by detours. Perhaps you've heard of the character Dennis Mitchell from *Dennis the Menace*? His name has become a synonym for the well-meaning child who has a way of turning perfect tranquility into perfect disaster.

We all turned to look at our mousey five-year-old standing in a suspiciously clean corner—she was our Dennis. Lindsey's head was lowered, eyes shifted sideways. She squirmed in a restrained way, hoping no one would notice her. I had a sudden flashback to the 1950s and the famous *I Love Lucy* moments when Ricky often said, "Lucy, you got some 'splainin' to do!"

Two parents' voices merged as we asked with exasperated sighs, "L-i-n-d-s-e-y, what have you done?"

Her lips were sealed, at least for the moment. Probably for the best—we all needed a bit of time.

Poor Lori, she'd had a good day, but a rough evening.

When you're out of school for an extended weekend and your morning begins with an Easter egg hunt, as well as a basket of goodies, that's a definite plus. Unfortunately, the evening had ended with her getting into trouble. The punishment was banishment to her bedroom, and you know how she woke up.

Over the next hour of cleanup, it became evident that Lori had experienced a night of thrashing. Some children sleepwalk if they go to bed upset. Not our girl—she was a thrasher and the wall had been her target. I scrubbed away hand and knee patterns, changed linens and checked on her periodically as she sobbed uncontrollably in the shower.

I heard the shower water stop. In a robe and head towel, Lori entered her room as a soldier to battle, shaky but in control. She sat on the edge of her freshly made bed. Lindsey sat down next to her. It looked like confession time. Clutching her stuffed bedtime bunny, Lindsey finally spoke.

"Sissy, remember how you got in trouble? I heard you crying until you went to sleep." Pointing to her chest, Lindsey said, "It hurt me in here when you cried. If you're sad, I'm sad, and when I'm sad, I always want my Beatrix Bunny to hug. So I took the big chocolate bunny out of your Easter basket and put it in your arms so we could both feel better. I love you, Sissy."

It was impossible to argue with her logic and after that explanation, forgiveness was a foregone conclusion. The beauty of a child's thinking, with all complexities stripped away, can certainly humble an adult.

The sisters hugged and kissed and my husband and I, hoping to avert any future repeat, did our best to explain body warmth and the concept of melting chocolate.

Twenty-five Easters have come and gone since then. Throughout the years, Lindsey has continued to live up to Dennis' legacy. Yes, it's been a wild ride, not one dull moment in our family. I must tell you that every spring since that fateful night, when chocolate bunnies line the store shelves, we all smile. And one of us will inevitably say, "What do you think? Should we stock up on some bunny love?"

Lori and Lindsey around the time of the incident

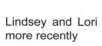

Lindsey and Lori more recently

# Dazed and Confused

by
Sallie Wagner Brown

My half-sisters are my only really interesting relatives, but they were not a large part of my life. Not only were they five to 20 years older than me, but most of the time, they lived in Idaho near their father's family.

I was raised by my father's sister in Salt Lake City, worlds apart, if not in distance, for sure in lifestyle. My half-sisters and I rarely got together for the holidays, but what encounters we had never lacked complication.

In my 16th summer, two of my half-sisters, each between husbands, were living together in Salt Lake City for a while. Feeling quite independent with my new driver's license, I dropped in one day hoping to borrow one of their cars. Their 16-year-old half-brother on their father's side was visiting from Idaho and had the same idea. Billy and I were never were quite able to figure out what our familial connection was, but we got along fine, probably because most of the family had such a sense of comedy about all the halves and steps.

Billy managed to snatch the car keys tossed to both of us, so he drove first. I could hardly wait for my turn.

Salt Lake City in the 1960s, like most big cities, had an unofficial drag strip. There, it was called USDM. Up State, Down Main. I'm sure the Mormon planners did not have fast cars and teenagers in mind when they designed the long, straight, wide streets progressing out from Temple Square, so orderly, so strategic. And they also probably did not expect Salt Lake to turn out to be less than 40 percent Mormon—an oasis of sinful normalcy in two states' worth of religious followers.

Our adventure had lasted less than three minutes when Billy missed the brake and rear-ended a much larger sedan in our sister's little silver Corvair. We'd gone only two blocks down Main Street.

"Now what?" He looked as if he thought I might actually have an answer as the policeman who'd materialized unbidden walked toward us.

"You could let me drive," I suggested helpfully.

He scowled at me as the policeman checked his driver's license and the car registration. There was only a moment's hesitation as Billy explained that his married sister's name on the registration would, of course, be different from his. The damage was minor, but we still got the mandatory sticker on the windshield of the car with the date and a short description of the incident. That record showed Billy as the driver at fault, an item he could be sure I would point out to our sibling-in-common. At least I was still having a good time.

It didn't take long for us to get in trouble again. We didn't notice the police car behind us as we waited at a stoplight, nose to nose with an old black Ford Victoria with its lowered front end. The boys in that car grinned but didn't look directly at us as the driver revved the engine. A Corvair doesn't produce a very impressive rev, but our apparent enthusiasm for the game made up for what the tiny car lacked. Billy hunched over the steering wheel with a toothy grin while I bounced in my seat.

The lights were flashing on the cop car before we even cleared the intersection. The Ford got away. Somehow, we were more interesting to the officers—and much easier to catch.

As one of them approached, I slid over next to Billy in order not to miss any of the fun. Billy already had his license and the car registration ready for the officer. He took the documents then, of course, asked who the owner of the car was. Both of us answered at the same time, "My sister." Big mistake.

He must have interpreted my position on the seat to mean that we were a couple, so he asked for my license, too, which only proved that Billy and I did not have the same last name as each other or as the registered owner of the car. It was about that time he noticed the accident sticker on the windshield.

With a gruff, "Stay here!" the officer walked back to his car to talk to his partner. I wasn't driving so I was still pretty amused, but Billy was getting a little worried. Our sister was not going to be happy. Worse yet, she was likely to tease us, especially him, about this for the rest of our lives.

"What do you think they'll do?"

I had no idea, but before I could come up with a smart-aleck response, both officers were at the car window and one of them wanted Billy to get out of the car. He got out very slowly, carefully showing his hands as he walked to the front of the police car where he leaned back against the fender to talk to the cop who had escorted him there.

Feeling a lot less smart-alecky, I started to get out of the car, too, but the other officer said I could just stay there. He seemed friendly enough as he put his hand on the door and looked down at the road. "OK. Who is the owner of the car?" he said in an offhand manner, smiling.

I liked him. "My sister."

"He says it belongs to his sister."

"It does. She's his sister, too."

"But he's not your brother."

"Uh, no."

He was looking less friendly and a lot more confused, so I continued.

"My sister has a different father who's also his father."

"What?"

"No, really. My sister and I have the same mother, but not the same father, but they have the same father."

"Who?"

I'm sure that if my children had to explain their adopted, step and half siblings today, it would go much more smoothly, but this was the 1960s, and we were in Utah. Marriages there usually don't even end when the couples die.

I hoped Billy was managing a more clear explanation than I was.

I tried again.

"OK. Many years ago, a woman was married to this man

and they had five daughters. Then they got a divorce. Both of them married someone else and they had more children with different fathers and mothers. Got it?"

Before he could attempt an answer, the other officer brought Billy back and told him to get into the car. They talked quietly for a minute then one of them said, "Just go directly back to where you got this car and give the keys to the owner, whoever she is. Don't let us see you on the road again. Got it?"

We got it, but I really don't think they ever did.

# The
# Later Years

---

Still acting up!

---

# Take Me Out to the Ballgame

by
Shari Courter

Something about our family draws attention. We joke that we're *The Truman Show*. Well, maybe we aren't joking. I think some part of us actually believes it's true. But when the crazy stuff that happens to us happens so often, it gets easier and easier to believe.

With baseball season approaching, I can't help but think of the Dayton Dragons. A minor league team, the Dragons are fun to watch because they're casual, family-oriented and very entertaining. Part of what makes the Dragons so unique is the silly games they play between innings with people picked right out of the crowd. But I'm getting ahead of myself.

Back in 2005, we went to a Dragons game for the very first time. We were running late that day, which is par for the course for our family whenever it involves my husband, Ron, and his addiction to finding a parking spot that involves the least amount of walking humanly possible. I suspect he never comes close to those 10,000 recommended steps per day, nor does he care to.

Once the coveted parking spot was found, Ron, our kids Zac, Aubrey and youngest daughter Kearstin and I ran to the entrance. That's when we were stopped by an employee. Not too surprising since we were dragging a six-year-old by her arm while we loudly cycled through a familiar argument involving words like "late," "parking" and "recommend 10,000 steps per day."

The employee asked if we would like to participate in a game between innings. Ron and I shot suspicious glances at each other, but she continued. She told us we would go down onto the field and the kids would get to go, too. That's when Zac, Aubrey and Kearstin weighed in on the decision with their excited, hopeful little faces. We had no choice but to agree. We were told to meet her after the third inning.

Needless to say, we didn't enjoy one minute of those first three innings. We were extremely nervous and both of us regretted what we had just agreed to—but, of course, we didn't even know what we had just agreed to. Ron finally pointed out that this was no big deal. It's not like we'd know anybody there so who cares what we do in front of thousands of strangers?

Not 10 minutes after he said that, a couple arrived late and began excusing themselves as they squeezed into our aisle to find their seats. They attend church with us. I glared at my husband. Not only did we know someone, but they were seated in our row! He finally admitted, "OK, those are bad odds."

When the time came, we slipped out of our seats as casually and discreetly as two large adults and three fighting children could. Which is to say that there was nothing casual and/or discreet about it and by the time we escaped the death glares of the people whose feet and legs we'd just trampled, our fellow spectators were practically applauding our early departure, hoping to never see us again. Little did they know . . .

The kids were separated from us and whisked up the field. Ron and I were led through a series of corridors down into the bowels of the stadium. When we got to the bottom, we saw another couple looking equally nervous. It is so true when they say that misery loves company, because we immediately felt better. Whatever it was we were about to do, we should only have 50 percent of the crowd's attention. At least that's what we told ourselves.

We were given costumes to wear. I had to wear a T-shirt that read, "Number One Mom." I just assumed that Ron would have a T-shirt that said, "Number One Dad." Imagine my shock when I came out of the dressing area to find him in a giant diaper—over the top of his jeans—with a bonnet on his head and carrying a huge baby bottle. His face was beet red and he was not a happy baby. Before he could blow his stack, we were quickly ushered out onto the field where two bright red Radio Flyer wagons were waiting by home plate.

Here was the deal: Ron and the other equally miserable and diapered man had to straddle the wagon while their wives pulled them around the baseline in a race. We were all starting at home plate. Ron and I would race toward the first base and the other couple would race toward the third base, we would pass each other somewhere around second base and whoever got back to home plate first won. Where were our kids, you might be wondering? They got to sit with the visiting team and the Dragons' mascot. They were loving it!

As gently as he could, Ron lowered himself onto the little wagon. The crowd was already laughing and so were the players of the Dragons team who were waiting in their positions on the field. In a panicked voice, Ron told me he thought he heard a cracking sound. I thought, *No way, big boy. That's a Radio Flyer. Those suckers are made of steel.*

Suddenly, we were told to go. I took off—or tried to— but because Ron's weight was toward the back of the wagon, as soon as I pulled, it tipped over and dumped him off the back. The word "crap"—or something along those lines—blurted out of my mouth when I saw the look on his face. But being the good sport that he is, he climbed back onto the wagon.

This time, I also heard a cracking sound. I started pulling the wagon down the baseline. To make it easier, I turned to face him so that I could use both hands to pull while I walked backward. I was trying to give reassuring smiles at my furious husband, but right before my eyes, I saw the wagon starting to fold up around his crotch like a bright red taco with his legs hanging out of the sides. Ron's eyes got huge when he felt the squeeze of the steel fold around him. To the credit of the Radio Flyer, it never did snap in half. But at least it would have put an end to this debacle. Instead, it folded in half until the wheels came slightly off the ground and the only thing touching the ground was the steel crease in the middle, thus leaving a trench of plowed dirt down the baseline as I pulled.

Somewhere behind me, I heard one of the Dragons players say, "Wow!" The crowd was going wild. That's the first time

I'd ever been on the receiving end of a crowd's roar and it was quite a rush. Gone were the hopes of only having half of the attention, because it's safe to say that every single eye was on us that day. The other couple easily won because somewhere between first and second base, our wagon became too deeply buried in dirt to be pulled.

The race was over and everything became a blur of activity as workers rushed out to repair the field for the next inning. Some guys who helped with the entertainment proudly displayed the broken wagon as they carried it around the field to the cheers of the crowd, while my husband yanked his diaper and bonnet off in a colossal temper tantrum. When we caught up with our kids in the visitors' dugout, the other team thanked us for the best thing they'd ever seen at a game and were kind enough to give our kids autographs.

It was finally time to return to our seats and regain anonymity as we blended back into the crowd to enjoy the rest of the game. No such luck. When we got back, our entire section gave us a standing ovation that lasted an awkward amount of time. Apparently these same people forgot that a mere 20 minutes ago they hated our very existence and cursed the day we were born for interrupting their game and possibly crushing several toes beyond recognition. When the game resumed, we joked that our 15 minutes of fame were over. What we didn't know was that minute 16 waited just around the corner.

One of the fun things they do during every game is name the "Fan of the Game." They flash three choices onto the giant screen, give them funny nicknames and let the crowd choose by applause. The screen was directly behind us, so we didn't even realize this was happening until we heard that familiar roar of the crowd. One of the three choices was Ron—a photo splashed across the screen of him in his bonnet and diaper, sitting in the middle of the curled-up wagon. The subtitle was "Man of Steel." The crowd went crazy and Ron won the honor of being selected the "Fan of the Game."

Ron's 15 minutes of fame was extended even further when the clip of our race made the team's highlight reel. For the next several years, anyone attending a Dragons game got to relive the fateful race.

Our family hasn't returned to a Dragons game since, but none of us will ever forget the year of the Draggin' Wagon. My husband is quick to remind everyone that they don't make Radio Flyers as strong as they used to.

Ron, Shari and the Draggin' Wagon!

# A Certain Air About Her

by

T'Mara Goodsell

She was the picture of a beautiful bride: a delicate, porcelain-skinned 23-year-old beauty whose flawless profile graced the portfolio of photographers around town.

My cousin Etta was so pretty, in fact, that when she visited New York City, several people asked for her autograph. They didn't know who she was, of course, but they figured that someone who looked like she did had to be somebody. And now Etta was out looking for a wedding dress—not to model for others this time, but to wear for her own upcoming Big Day.

If people had known about her true talent, would they still have asked for her autograph? I have to wonder, because they were right, in a sense. Etta was somebody . . . somebody whose flatulence was the stuff of which legends are made. Really, really stinky legends.

My cousin Etta had a secret time bomb ticking within her.

A stink bomb. Etta had the most offensive flatulence ever. It was a talent, really. It wasn't simply the withering intensity of the odor, but its sheer ability to seem to create an ever-expanding mushroom cloud of putrefaction which traveled, overcoming unsuspecting people for acres and acres in its deadly invisible cloud. Oh, not everyone knew about her talent. She worked hard to keep it from polite society, such as our parents. But impolite society, such as we cousins, knew that Etta's intestinal gas was almost weapons-grade.

It hit the proverbial fan one day when I was invited to go along on a shopping trip for Etta's wedding gown. The saleslady led Etta, Aunt Lily and me into some gilded and chandeliered catacombs positively engorged with endless white fluffery. As I strolled through those miles and miles of pristine poufs and heirloom lace, it was as if a dead-silent stink grenade suddenly blew up in my face. I immediately turned to Etta so that our eyes could have the too-familiar argument: *Here? Really? You couldn't have waited?*

And Etta's large green eyes clearly expressed: *I wasn't expecting it to be this bad. Please, please, please! Don't give me away!*

Then Aunt Lily was hit by the fallout. "Good heavens! What is that dreadful smell?!" Etta's eyes got more desperate: *Pleeeeeeease DON'T TELL!*

Etta had outdone herself this time. This stench truly did rise to the occasion, enveloping everything around it with the foul gas. Aunt Lily didn't help the situation any. She was a thin woman who was sensitive to unpleasant odors. She couldn't stand certain restaurants that served fish. Public restrooms had to be approached with caution. She began—not quite so delicately—to gag.

She turned to the saleslady and demanded to know what was going on with her store. The poor woman, of course, looked horrified and baffled. She assured us that she had never in her life smelled such a thing before.

"Oh, mercy!" Aunt Lily exclaimed. "Oh, horrors!" She dry-heaved. She waved. She flailed. "A sewer line must have broken. You need to call someone!" She donned protective gear in the form of her embroidered white hanky and took out the smelling salts that she carried for just such emergencies and waved them dramatically about.

My eyes watered from both the stench and the effort to keep from laughing. I broke out in a sweat and concentrated on my shoes. The problem was, the odor was trapped in what was essentially a long closet. One could only hope that it was ricocheting off the plastic-draped frippery like frou-frou foosball. There was no way out for it, so all we could do was cover our faces and run for the nearest exit.

Aunt Lily pronounced the store off limits, saying she ought to report this to the store manager! My cousin agreed—but after I shot her a look almost as withering as the odor, she added that perhaps it was best to walk out. So we did, as indignantly as possible.

Shortly after that, we heard that the entire department store was closing down forever. Oh, they said they'd gone out of business. Those of us who knew Etta knew the real reason.

# Nana Got the Last Word

by
Mona Dawson

My dad had his classic 1967 Chevy Impala tuned up. It was truly a hot car—beige, sleek and a quiet ride. If decorated properly with great rims, he would have been the envy of all lowriders. As it was, it was classy and cool. And with its big V8 engine, it was fast.

It was spring break and Mom and my grandmother Nana were going to Nana's house in Pacific Grove, just off California's magnificent coastline and adjacent to Monterey. Since school was out, Mom wanted my family to join them, so I packed up the boys and the five us took off in this hot, cool car, loaded with a week's worth of gear. And I drove. Since I normally drove a small Opal, I now felt like I was driving the Queen Mary. I think the car actually floated.

For anyone not knowing my mom or Nana or what wild boys I had, it's hard for me to describe the immediate noise level in the car. But for those who know us, let me just say that

I could see the head shaking and the eye-rolling glances of my friendly neighbors as we pulled out of my driveway. I'd like to think they felt sorry for me, but more likely they were looking forward to a quiet week in the neighborhood.

Mom had a naturally loud voice. But she was also hard of hearing. Vanity prevented her from admitting it, so she spoke much louder than necessary. The boys never stopped talking and because they wanted to be heard over my mom's voice, they kicked up their volume, as well.

Nana and my mom disagreed on practically everything, so they pretty much fought nonstop. In fact, they were worse than my boys, who even fought with each other in their sleep.

As the drive progressed, the noise level in the car went up and down as I kept asking everyone to stop fighting and not to talk so loudly. But naturally, they couldn't hear me. And I was trying to stay calm and not lose my temper because this was supposed to be a good trip for all of us, a fun getaway. Pacific Grove was the best place on earth for such an adventure.

We were heading south on Highway 101, my grip on the wheel tight, and my neck and shoulders hurting. The volume of everyone in the car was getting to me, and I was a little tense, to put it mildly. The car had a quiet, smooth ride and no outside noise could be heard, but I was certain the noise inside the car caused it to vibrate. The boys were jumping around in the back seat—there was no seat-belt law at the time. Mom sat in the front seat next to me and argued with Nana, who was in the back seat, which pumped up the volume even more. It made me wonder why in the heck I had agreed to this and whether I would ever do it again. The answer was, "NO!"

"Everyone, please keep the noise down," I kept saying,

taking deep breaths. I was going more than 75 mph, and when they got quieter, my foot eased off the gas pedal. The louder they got, the heavier my foot got. I know, right? It's science— the louder the noise, the heavier the foot, the greater the speed.

Soon after my last plea, a highway patrol car appeared beside me. He came out of nowhere. I couldn't believe I hadn't seen him. But then, I couldn't believe four generations in one car could be so much trouble either. He pointed at me then at the side of the road with an angry look. I guess that meant pull over.

"$%^!" I mumbled under my breath, just like my dad.

"What's wrong?" my mom snapped.

"I'm getting pulled over. I think I was going more than 75 mph. Damn, I've never had a ticket in my life."

I told everyone to be quiet and let me talk. I'd talked myself out of tickets three times before, so I hoped I could do it again now. The boys got really quiet and sat still, and for some reason they were a little afraid, but not Mom and Nana. They couldn't stop fighting with each other. Each blamed the other for making too much noise.

"See, I told you to be quiet," one said.

"NO, I told YOU to be quiet," the other replied.

"Quiet!" I yelled. "Nobody talk!"

The cop was built like a mountain. He had to be at least 6 feet 6 inches tall and weighed 250 pounds—he towered over the Impala. I felt like he could squash us. I rolled my window down and looked up at the mountain of a man with total despair on my face. Mom and Nana were still yelling at each other, playing the blame game.

He looked down at me and spoke softly. "Didn't you see me? I've been following you for five miles."

"No, I'm sorry, I didn't see you. I'm having trouble keeping the noise level down. Between my mom, my grandmother and my boys, I'm having trouble focusing on the speed. I'm sorry, really. I didn't see you at all."

"Well, your boys did. They've been waving at me, laughing and jumping up and down. I was sure they would have warned you."

I turned purple with rage as I turned and looked at my boys. "You saw the officer and didn't tell me?"

They sat there, scared, heads down and just nodded.

"We thought he was playing with us," the older one said.

Oh yeah, great. A cop follows you because he's bored and needs to play. Nice. I decided I'd kill them both later.

"Can I see your license and registration, please? Did you know you were going more than 70?"

"Yes. Once I saw you next to me, I looked at the speedometer. I am sorry, I didn't realize this car could go so fast. It was recently tuned up," I said, thinking how stupid that sounded.

I reached for the glove compartment, but now my mom got in the way.

"Officer, it's our fault, not hers. She's been asking us to keep the noise down, but we just kept talking."

"Talking?" he asked. He looked at my mom then to my grandmother. "I could hear your screaming voices before I got out of my car. I'm surprised she could drive at all. And you boys should be ashamed of yourselves. Driving is serious business and your mom needs to concentrate. You'd better sit down and be quiet back there."

I handed him the license and registration, and as he started to walk away, I let out a sigh of relief. "I think he might let me go with just a warning," I whispered. He had seemed very sympathetic toward me, and even tried to conceal a smile.

And that's when it happened. Nana just couldn't keep her mouth shut.

"GOOD!" she yelled after him from her spot in the back seat. "He'd better let us go. How dare he stop us! Who does he think he is?"

My heart stopped, and my head went down when I glanced in my side mirror and saw the mountain of a man stop dead in his tracks. He turned and slowly walked back to the car. He leaned way down and looked at my grandmother in the back seat.

"Excuse me, ma'am. What did you say?"

"Yooou!" she growled at him slowly, pointing a crooked arthritic finger at him. "You just ruined my granddaughter's perfect driving record. She's never had a ticket in her life and now you've ruined it."

He stood, unbuckled the pad from the hook on his belt, flipped it open, clicked open his ballpoint pen and quietly replied, "I'm not the one who ruined her record."

And he began writing my first speeding ticket.

The infamous Impala

# What Goes Around Comes Around

by
### Glady Martin

I was a real prankster in my early 20s. But I became more daring with age—I had less fear of going too far with my jokes.

My sister-in-law and my mother-in-law were usually my victims because they were a little like me, and I knew that they would be able to take what I dished out. Oh, how we had fun laughing over the reactions of my bag of gifts and tricks. It was also very entertaining for our families. I really don't know how they put up with it for so many years.

I finally began slowing down on my clowning around because I needed some fresh material and was all out of ideas. Besides, Darlene and Mom Edith were such ladies that there was only so much a gagster could do without getting too frisky.

As it turned out, my funny bone grew numb due to some serious health problems and needed emergency major surgery. I knew this would dampen my spirits, but, at the very least, it would give my family a welcome reprieve from my antics.

I lay in the hospital bed after surgery, moaning and groaning in pain. Getting up and down was very difficult because I had a huge "smiley face" incision on my abdomen. How fitting that the surgeon would mark me for eternity with a frozen grin below the belt. I wondered if Darlene had spoken to the doc and asked him to do so!

On the fourth day of recovery, I was able to get up and down from my bed by myself. The pain was still very raw and I was still receiving "happy shots" every four hours. On this day, the nurse gave me my shot 40 minutes earlier than the regular time. I tried to question her about it, but by the time the liquid raced through my veins and made my eyelids heavy and my tongue thick, all that came out was, "Gal be da tru gad low." I decided I wasn't going to even try to communicate with anyone. I didn't mind making a fool out of others, but I sure as heck wasn't going to make a fool out of myself!

My roommate was a lovely little Asian woman and she didn't speak English and didn't talk much so I was happy to just drift into la-la land.

Suddenly, my sleep was disturbed by a commotion down the hall. It sounded like someone was angry.

"How dare they speak so loudly! Don't they know that there are sick people in here?"

Two "ladies of the night" entered my room. It was Mom Edith and Darlene dressed as hookers! My sweet little mother-in-law and my very intellectual sister-in-law were dressed to the nines, adorned with net stockings, miniskirts, cleavage and stilettos. Their hair was backcombed so high it would have made Chewbacca from *Star Wars* jealous. Their red lips and bright eye shadow was another story. And oh, they were saying things that would embarrass a dog.

"Where is that girl? She has been here long enough. I am sick and tired of taking over her corner and working my corner at the same time! I am plum tired, and here she is on her back with all these handsome doctors coming in and out of her room. Glady, you get yourself out and work your own corner!"

I began laughing hysterically. Still goofy from my shot, I couldn't stop laughing. I held my stapled tummy. Talk about busting a gut! In my mind, I was yelling, *Help! Stop! I'm in trouble!*

Even if I had been shouting aloud, no one would have heard me because the doctors and nurses were standing in the doorway, all laughing, as well. All I could do was laugh and snort along with them.

After everyone settled down and I gathered my senses, my family members confessed they had called the hospital and forewarned them they were coming to repay me for the many years of pranks I had pulled on them. I shouldn't complain too much. They did inquire whether the laughing would cause any damage to my stapled incision. That's why the doctor had ordered an early pain shot.

Shortly thereafter, the staff went back to work. That's when my roommate's husband came in. Well, you should have seen his eyeballs when he saw two hookers at my bedside! His wife gave him one good slap on his back.

Later, when it was just myself and my roommate, I tried explaining to her that it was all a joke. She sneered at me and pulled her book up to cover her face. Then I remembered that she didn't speak English—I can only imagine what she thought of my family's prank.

Trust me, what goes around, comes around. And now that I'm back to feeling better, it's time to get even. Watch out, my loving family!

# Close, But No Cigar

by
Debra Ayers Brown

I thought I'd made myself clear when allowing my cousins to stay in Mama's vacant house for a few months after Papa's death, although I should have been getting it ready to sell. It had been difficult to take care of the house after she'd moved five hours away to live with us. Perhaps it would help to have her niece living there, even if I didn't know her children or grandchildren. Besides, how could I say no? Our large family always got involved—wanted or not.

So I'd agreed to the temporary living arrangement with one caveat, which I explained to them during several phone calls: "No cigarettes, no cigars and no funny stuff. I don't want the furniture and carpet to reek of smoke." That's why I was surprised when the old house had gone from a "no smoking" zone to a pot-growing zone.

According to the family grapevine, one of Mama's neighbors told my cousin, who informed my uncle, who told Mama we had marijuana plants growing everywhere at the old house.

"You've got to be kidding," I said, going into panic mode when I found out. I paced the floor, recalling the distinct, pungent odor surrounding stoners during my college days. I also remembered how they'd lurked in the shadows with a customer, selling weed they'd grown in their rooms.

I thought to myself, *Oh. My. God. My cousins aren't just using it—they're selling it!*

Heaven help me. What would my hubby say when the Feds seized Mama's house for drugs? I'd have to fess up that, thanks to me, enough relatives to fill up a holding cell had occupied the house for months. And what about our teetotaler, Bible-toting, born-and-raised-Southern relatives? They'd come together for weddings, holidays, reunions and even an intervention. But they'd have a hissy fit about an illegal drug operation.

And what about Mama? She already missed Papa and their home of more than 60 years in the rolling hills of North Georgia. She grieved for both—and for her close-knit family and friends still living there. Could she survive grief and gossip and scandal?

The enormity of the situation sickened me.

I tossed and turned through a fitful night while every possible scenario flashed before me. In the dark hours before dawn, I accepted my part in the fiasco. If I hadn't been such a soft touch, selling furniture and listing the house would have been our biggest worries. Now, I'd sullied the family name and we'd be disowned.

Could Mama escape a second heart attack? I could see her obituary even in my dream: "From a family of nine children, the deceased is survived by three brothers and two sisters, all

God-fearing, law-abiding community members. She leaves behind a son-in-law, a beloved granddaughter and an only daughter who caused her great disappointment in her final days. In lieu of flowers, friends may make donations to the bail bondsman for said daughter who will receive condolences at the county jail where she temporarily resides. Editor's note: The crime family is suspected of working with the Cuban cartel in the state's largest drug operation to date. Mrs. Brown claims her innocence, but how could she not know about 1,000 pot plants growing in her mother's home? Puh-lease."

I awoke with a start. I'd actually killed Mama off. Next stop, a *Dateline* exclusive titled "Debutante Dances Around Drugs" which was better than "Debbie Does Dallas," but not by much. Somehow, I pulled myself together enough to shower and get ready for work.

As I drove to work in a foggy haze, my entire life sentence passed before me, and a new seedling of fear stoked the fire. My pulse raced. I watched the rear-view mirror for blue lights. In an instant, my face could be slammed against the window, handcuffs whipped out and snapped around my delicate wrists, binding hands not accustomed to any real physical labor. Was an orange jumpsuit in my future? A 12-step program? Worse yet, would the family block me on Facebook?

In my paranoid state, I felt drugged. The authorities must be waiting for me at work. I could imagine how an interrogation would go down. I'd have to explain my red eyes. Would they understand I'd had a restless night, skipped breakfast and needed some Coke? Good grief! I hoped the Feds would realize I meant Coca Cola, preferably diet.

I snapped out of the paranoia when I decided to plead the fifth about anything pertaining to marijuana, cannabis, reefer, pot or Mary Jane.

As I drove the rest of the way to work, I remained silent, envisioning rows of plants in 5-gallon buckets in every room in Mama's rambling ranch, now equipped with grow lights, irrigation, ventilation and climate control for a perfect temperature of 87 degrees. Why did I ever agree to rent to my cousins?

I needed advice from our attorney. Maybe the accountant could prove we had no new money. But all I really wanted was my mama.

And Mama's who I got when her name displayed on my ringing iPhone. I answered with, "We have to get the pot out of your house."

"What are you talking about?"

I repeated what her neighbor told my cousin, who informed my uncle, who told her, and then me about pot growing everywhere.

Mama laughed. "You're close, but no cigar," she said. "Marijuana plants were growing everywhere in my *neighbor's* mom's house."

I almost cried, relieved that my cousins weren't growing weed in and dealing drugs from Mama's house. Then I realized where the neighbor's mom lived—a few doors down from Mama.

"I empathize with them," I said with sincerity. "But drugs in the neighborhood will probably bring down the value of your house." I could almost see Mama's stricken face. Wanting to reassure her, I said, "Don't worry, Mama. At least we don't have to deal with cigarettes or cigars—only the funny stuff."

# When There's a Will . . .

by
**Verna Simms**

Come the end of spring, I was so looking forward to June, my favorite month of the year. All nature comes alive, fragrant flowers bloom with delightful aromas and fully leafed trees spread foliage of various shades of green. Pretty birds spread their wings and glide from trees to nests. Love is in the air. Sunshine caresses my skin. But most importantly, this year my mother would be celebrating her 90th birthday.

I had big plans for Mother's special day. Most of my siblings and their families were scattered across the United States, but that was no reason not to have a huge birthday cake. I'd recently learned to make pretty roses with cake icing and decided to make a circle of roses and splash 90 colorful candles in the center of her cake. It would be gorgeous. Her small party would be fun.

Then Mother became seriously ill. Her doctor said to her, "Mrs. Hill, if you won't agree to a gallbladder operation, you must follow a very strict diet for the rest of your life."

Mother chose the diet. I took her to my home and slowly ran my finger down the smooth white paper reading the long list of forbidden foods. My finger stuck like glue at the fateful word "cake" and my heart sank. *What to do? No cake means no candles. Or does it?* I thought to myself. I racked my brain. Surely I could think of something that would hold 90 lit candles.

"Quit fretting, honey," my husband, Howard, said. "Buy her a dozen roses and serve sherbet—she's allowed that, isn't she? Anyway, I never cared for the idea of old people blowing their germs on something I plan to eat."

I nodded, but still moped around the house, trying hard to hide my disappointment.

Then an idea came to me. *Why not?* I told no one about my plan.

As the big birthday approached, I purchased birthday napkins, plates and three boxes of small candles. Howard raised his eyebrows but said nothing. Perhaps he was relieved to see me out of my funk.

On Mother's birthday, I set the table, placing a vase of nine deep-yellow roses at one end and at the other end, I placed a basket crammed with ferns and clusters of fragrant blossoms cut from foliage growing in Mother's yard. I knew the aroma would mask the liniment Mother used for her arthritis.

On a white tablecloth, in the very center of the beautifully decorated table, I placed a large silver tray. An enormous, oval, deep-green watermelon rested on the tray. With an ice pick, I poked 90 holes into the rind and placed a small birthday candle into each.

It was more difficult than I had anticipated, but when I saw the look of surprise and pleasure on Mother's face, I knew the effort had been well worth it. Her soft brown eyes brightened like a child's at Christmas. We sang "Happy Birthday" and I snapped a picture as Mother puckered her lips, took a deep breath and blew. It took three tries, but she extinguished all 90 flames on her birthday watermelon.

Mom with her birthday watermelon, which, for safety, was moved to the kitchen for the candle lighting!

# Payback's a Bitch

by
Terri Duncan

My 40th birthday was rapidly approaching, but it couldn't have come at a more inconvenient time in my life.

I had imagined that by the time I turned the big 4-0, I would own a hot-red sports car, have unlimited time to travel and all the money I needed to live a comfortable life. Instead, my husband and I found ourselves suddenly starting over. The company where he had worked for almost 20 years was closing its local facility and we were faced with a bleak, uncertain future.

Because it appeared that I would have to become the primary breadwinner, I returned to college to obtain an advanced degree to increase my income potential. The funny thing was that my fellow students were all far younger than I was. During this time, I also searched for a higher-paying job. My husband, who was constantly scanning the want ads in hopes of finding a new career, also decided to return to college. Between school costs, our monthly budget and preparation for the unknown, finances were tight. There were neither sports cars nor trips to exotic locals in our immediate future.

As my birthday drew closer, I made it very clear to my family—especially my brother and sister—that I didn't want any hoopla. Instead, I wanted the day to pass quietly and un-eventfully. I didn't want any reminders of what "should have been" on my 40th birthday.

While my husband, children and mother respected my wishes, I should have known my brother and sister would not let an opportunity like my 40th pass without incident. How naïve of me to believe that my siblings would not secretly plan something to commemorate the event!

We three siblings are close in age and have always searched for excuses to plot and plan. We grew up in a neighborhood with few children our age, so it was just us. Together, we built forts and tree houses in the woods and even constructed im-penetrable dams across the creek behind our house. And after reading the *Foxfire* books that were popular in the 1970s, we decided to build our own moonshine still, despite the fact that we had no idea what moonshine was.

As we grew older we continued to plot and plan, though the ulterior motives differed from those of our younger years. We double-dated and occasionally triple-dated, and every once in a while, we covered for each other when explaining to our parents the reason for breaking curfews. We kept secrets among ourselves. I promised my brother never to mention the little incident that occurred while leaving school one day a little too rapidly, and my siblings and I agreed not to bring up that little run-in at the lake with friends. Ours was a trio that was one for all and all for one.

Of course, there were times—40th birthdays, for instance—

when the plotting and planning involved two of the three of us, all at the expense of the one left out. My sister was the first to turn 40, so my brother and I secretly stole to her house in the dark of night and planted 40 pink plastic flamingos adorned with Christmas lights in her front yard to remind her and all her neighbors of her special day. With this latest prank in mind, I worried that the two of them would cook up some plan to get me on my big day.

The first clue that something was up came when the telephone rang very early on my birthday morning, when I was still asleep. At first, I thought that my body was betraying me—here I was, barely 40, and I was already hearing a ringing noise in my head! When I finally realized that it was the phone and not my aging ears, I answered and heard the familiar voice of an old business associate on the other end wishing me a happy birthday. Groggily, I listened and thanked him, but then it occurred to me that he had never called me on my birthday before. In fact, how did he know I was turning 40? So I asked him.

"Well, sugar," he drawled, "I saw the sign out on the highway!"

I sat up in the bed, now wide-awake. What in the world was he talking about? I quickly hung up and yelled for my husband and children. They bounded into the room, full of smiles and good cheer. I demanded to know what they had done. All three swore they had not participated in any sign-making endeavors. Their surprised faces convinced me they were indeed innocent. Then, the telephone rang again. I picked it up and was greeted by my little brother's loud guffaw.

"Hey, old lady!" he shouted. "So, you were able to hobble to the phone, huh?"

And that is when I knew who the culprits were—my brother and sister! I demanded to know where this sign was advertising to the world that I was now officially a middle-aged woman. This brought another round of laughter from my dear, sweet brother.

"You might want to take a drive down the road, old lady," he said. "There's a whole lot more than one sign out there on the street!"

*Crap!* I screamed to myself. I quickly hung up, grabbed my car keys and raced out of the house in my housecoat, night-gown and slippers. Despite my 40 years, I convinced myself that if I moved quickly enough, I could muster up some damage control.

That's when I saw the first sign. There were birthday messages written in vibrant colors all over my car! My name and age were visible for all to see. Knowing that the early morning light would hamper the ability of passersby to decipher the messages on the car, I jumped in and raced down the driveway.

That's when I saw the second sign, at the end of our long driveway. It was yet another 40th birthday announcement! However, the poster-sized sign mounted on the mailbox for my neighbors' viewing pleasure was not as bad as I expected. It would just have to wait until I got home.

The urgent matter racing through my head was the larger public display my old business associate had seen on the highway. I sped through the neighborhood, and then there it was, at the entrance off the highway into our subdivision—a huge banner announced my birthday, for all to see. I didn't know whether to laugh or cry. So much for dismissing my birthday!

Whether I wanted to ignore it or not, my brother and sister had made certain that I would be acknowledged.

As the sun slowly rose in the morning sky, I came to my senses enough to realize that it wouldn't be appropriate for a middle-aged woman to attempt to get the large banner down while in her nightgown. That would certainly be a more embarrassing public display. I couldn't help but smile at my sibling's antics. *Maybe 40 isn't too bad after all*, I told myself.

When I walked back into the house, the telephone was once again ringing. This time, it was my sister who was a bit kinder in her greeting. After all, she had already reached that 40-year milestone. Together, we laughed at the display I saw on the main road and she reminded me I had it coming after the little flamingo incident.

Before hanging up, I assured her that the sign at the entrance to the neighborhood would be coming down very quickly as soon as I was dressed in proper banner-removing attire.

"Sign?" she asked innocently. "Don't you mean 'signs?' Um, you might want to drive a little farther down the road." The two of them had plastered the entire area with signs announcing my landmark birthday.

All day long, I received birthday wishes from friends, neighbors, acquaintances and even the mailman who had seen the two massive banners proclaiming, "Lordy, lordy, Terri Duncan is 40!" I also learned that my brother was the mastermind and financier behind the birthday signage plan, but I have forgiven his trespasses. After all, he turns 40 soon. My sister and I have been plotting and planning for months because as the old saying goes, payback's a bitch.

# CHAPTER THREE

# Mind Your Table Manners

Someone's always stirring the pot.

# Getting Our Just Desserts

by
Lisa Tognola

My Aunt Jo used to say, "Don't bite the hand that feeds you." She uttered that phrase any time we complained or didn't seem grateful for something she did for us. She always expected respect be given for the respect she tendered.

I can still remember the day when we cousins, grown and with kids of our own, put her favorite saying to the test. The table was filled with the usual overabundance of holiday foods. We had just started to fill our plates with seconds when Aunt Jo jumped up from the table and scurried into the kitchen.

"I almost forgot something!" she yelled from the depths of the refrigerator.

*What could she have forgotten?* I wondered. My eyes scanned the table which was brimming with a 20-pound turkey and all the veritable fixings—stuffing with meat and without, cranberry sauce whole and jellied, three kinds of vegetables and potatoes mashed, twice-stuffed and candied.

Before I could wager a guess, she was back. She held a small salad plate piled with some sort of white food that had a swollen, bulb-like base.

"What's that?" my husband asked.

"This," she said, with dramatic pause, "is anus!"

I stopped mid-bite, turkey leg in hand. The room fell under a stunned silence. Parents, grandparents, kids and cousins all exchanged wild glances.

"It's what?" my husband choked.

"It's anus," she repeated, placing the plate on the table. Everyone leaned in for a closer look.

"The clerk at the store said if you cut the anus, it releases a strong scent. It's supposed to smell like black licorice." She broke off a piece of what by now we had figured out to be fresh anise, or as some know it, fennel. "Smell the anus," she insisted. The entire table broke into hysterics. I glanced up at Aunt Jo, who looked mildly humored, but in a confused way.

My husband reached for a piece of anise and popped it into his mouth. "Mmmm—best anus I've ever had!" Laughter exploded and our teenage son cracked up so hard that no sound came from his mouth.

"What happens if you squeeze the anus?" someone quipped. And the jokes continued nonstop.

At this point, I was rolling on the floor, unable to take in air. Aunt Jo remained unaware, trying to ignore the nonsense going on around her. Finally, my uncle ushered her into the other room. They whispered back and forth. She nodded then blushed crimson with embarrassment.

When she returned, her high heels clicking with the determination of each step, we hurried to compose ourselves. This time, she didn't have to say, "Don't bite the hand that feeds you." We could see it written all over her face.

"Help yourselves to the A-NISE (an´is)," Aunt Jo announced with a deliberate purpose, "because tonight there is no pie."

Suddenly, I remembered Aunt Jo's second favorite phrase growing up. With shameful acceptance, I realized that she was holding back the pie in order to give us what we had coming to us—we were "finally getting our just desserts."

# Food Fighters

by
Jenny Beatrice

I grew up surrounded by a gaggle of gourmets, my mother being one of the finest in the family. Our daily dinner menu ranged from quiche Lorraine to beer batter fish and chips, from Cornish hens to fettuccine Alfredo. And holidays—forget about it! Mom had a banquet prepared for every season. She was best known for her St. Patrick's Day corned beef and cabbage, drawing in family, friends and parish priests from miles around.

But of all her dishes, her true specialty was serving my dad a mean plate of whoop-ass. You would think that in a family full of Irish and Italian yellers, the colorful language and obscene hand gestures were enough to get the point across. But Mom took it a step further. No matter the fight, she wanted the last word. When she ran out of words, she resorted to throwing food. And not just any food—meat. It was a carnivorous expression of her rage for which I'm sure Sigmund Freud has a name.

My favorite food fight was rather one-sided. It happened when I was a teenager. After a busy day of school and teenage whatnot, I arrived home late and had missed dinner. The kitchen was clean, but two hamburgers remained in wait in a warm frying pan. I grabbed one and went to the family room to eat it in front of the TV. By the time I went to get the second one, the pan was empty. I shrugged it off and returned to my reruns.

A few minutes later, I heard Dad bellowing from the basement, "What is this?! What the hell is this?!" I ran to the top of the stairs to see what the fuss was about. I saw what looked like a brown ball on the floor by Dad's feet. We looked at each other, totally confused. Then, from the bedroom, Mom chimed in. "It's a hamburger. I threw that at you, I threw THAT at YOU!"

Dad mumbled, shook his head and walked away, leaving the ground chuck behind. Neither one of us ever figured out why she did it, and she never offered an explanation.

Mom wasn't the first food fighter in her family. She learned the trade from her mother, who was also a legend in the kitchen and in the ring. Grandma never missed preparing a fully cooked meal, no matter the circumstance. So even while recovering from a boob job—yes, a boob job—she decided to whip up a leg of lamb for dinner. Somehow, she still had the energy to bicker with Grandpa, and an argument came to a full-boil.

With her upper body in pain and her arms stuck to her sides, she picked up the lamb with all her might and tried to fling it at Grandpa. Just like a tyrannosaurus rex filled with great fury but built with tiny arms, she could only propel the lamb a few inches, so it fell straight to the floor.

Grandpa laughed. "What are you doing?" he asked.

And straight from the playbook, Grandma said, "I'm throwing this at you." And another dinner bit the dust.

Grandpa had a way of making all the women in the family mad, including my mother. One time he ticked her off while she was preparing the evening's pork chops. Something he said compelled her to throw that raw meat on the floor with so much force that it flattened the chop perfectly, just as if Julia Child had tenderized it with a mallet. Bon appetite!

When I left home for college, I was no longer witness to many of these food fights, but I didn't doubt they were still going on. So when I had to bring my fiancé, Bob (who is now my husband) into the mix, I feared it would be a recipe for disaster. Bob was quite impressed with Mom's cooking and looked forward to visiting, but he didn't know about the danger. Was he quick enough to dodge a flying filet mignon? Would he still marry me after getting whacked with a beef Wellington?

Well, it didn't take long to find out. One day, Bob, Mom and I were in the kitchen preparing a lunch of deli delights, happily spreading mayo onto bread and slicing tomatoes. Dad came into the house and the battle started between him and Mom, cutting our happiness like a knife. After a few minutes of top-of-your-lungs arguing, things moved to a broil. Dad left the room and Mom was left to stew with us and the deli meat. And then it happened.

Mom started rapid-fire throwing the ham and turkey around the kitchen. The meat clung to the cabinets, slowly slipping down the dark wood like those sticky wall crawlers you get from gumball machines. To my surprise, Bob didn't run out the door screaming. More surprisingly, neither did I. We waited patiently for the meat to land on our white and wheat and finished lunch. That was the day I knew Bob was a keeper.

Thankfully, the Meat Ninja gene stopped there. I do not throw meat or meat by-products. I also don't cook. I just don't take after my maternal side in these ways. For example, Mom can't remember what any of these fights were about in the first place. I, on the other hand, remember the reason behind every stink eye Bob and I ever made. Maybe I should start throwing food as a catharsis, clearing the memories of disagreements. It could be good for my marriage. And my waistline.

Two vivacious food fighters!

# From Soup to Putz

by
Mike McHugh

One thing that I'll always remember about Uncle Jack is that he could cook a mean pot of crab soup. Maryland style— the only way to do it as far as he was concerned—with lots of fresh vegetables, halves of backfin and claws still in the shell. Bisque was simply not his bag. "Just a fancy name the French people came up with so they can feel good about eating baby food," he'd say.

Uncle Jack's crab soup was legendary. He'd spend all day in the kitchen at the Knights of Columbus hall cooking up 50-gallon batches for their annual crab feast. And he never used a recipe. The soup would be gone before the affair was half over. On one occasion, when the pot began running low exceptionally early, Uncle Jack caught the event chairperson trying to water it down. The man learned a lesson that day—a stainless steel ladle in Uncle Jack's hands carries the power of Thor's mighty hammer.

As good as his soup was, Uncle Jack was always modest about his culinary ability. Whenever I'd pass along to him the many compliments I'd heard about his soup, he'd brush them off, saying, "Oh, you could put a horse turd on a lettuce leaf and this crowd would eat it."

Uncle Jack may have downplayed his skill, but we—his family—were grateful. I recall many summer days during my childhood when we'd gather at the apartment he shared with his sister, my Aunt Rita, for a bushel of steamed crabs and his soup.

Neither Uncle Jack nor Aunt Rita ever married, so they lived together their entire lives. That's one thing I envy about Uncle Jack even more than his soup—how he was able to share a place with his sister all that time in relative peace. Putting my sister and me together would be like Martha Stewart rooming with Larry the Cable Guy.

Their living arrangement was not always cool breeze and sunshine, however. For example, there was the incident involving jockey shorts. Aunt Rita worked for a dealer who leased cars to a number of players for the Baltimore Orioles. One of the clients was Hall-of-Fame pitcher Jim Palmer, who was also a model for Jockey underwear. One day while visiting the dealership, Jim Palmer gifted her with a pair of autographed shorts. Aunt Rita was a huge fan of his and was elated at receiving this odd treasure.

"What in the hell are you going to do with those?" Uncle Jack chided when she brought them home.

"I'm thinking about hanging them on top of the Christmas tree this year," she told him.

Uncle Jack didn't fancy the idea of having a pair of men's underwear hanging around in the apartment. Luckily, crab season comes in summer, thus we were all spared the indigestion that such a display would surely have caused among the male element of our clan.

The traditional way to prepare crabs in Maryland is to steam them whole with lots of Old Bay Seasoning—a local, red-pepper-based concoction. You spread newspaper across the table and dump the hot crabs in a pile in the middle. It takes no small amount of work with a wooden mallet and a table knife to get to the meat. You expend more calories hammering at the shells than you do eating the meat once you've exposed it. Our country's obesity problem would be solved if the fast-food restaurants made it as hard to get at their double-patty hamburgers.

Uncle Jack and my father operated on their crabs with surgical precision. My brothers and I were more like the comedian Gallagher with his Sledge-o-Matic at a produce stand. If crab shells were shrapnel, my mom and Aunt Rita would have been awarded Purple Hearts. Mom yelled scathing remarks at us for splattering crab guts all over the place. I offered to wipe them up with Jim Palmer's undershorts. Aunt Rita was not amused.

Clearly, eating steamed crabs is a messy affair. In addition to all of the shells and guts, you end up getting Old Bay all over your hands. For this reason, Maryland leads the nation in consumption of paper towels per capita, a leading cause of global deforestation, outranking paper wasted by law offices. And even with all those paper towels, it's impossible to keep your hands clean of the peppery gook. This is why when eating steamed crabs, it's critical to wash your hands thoroughly before engaging in certain other activities. My youngest brother learned this lesson the hard way.

What with all those spices, Dad and Uncle Jack considered eating crabs a perfect excuse to drink lots of beer, leading to frequent nature calls. On this particular occasion, nature had a bullhorn in my father's ear. Unfortunately, when he went to the apartment's only bathroom, he found it was occupied.

Dad was admirably stoic. However, after several minutes of shifting in his seat as if a sea nettle were lodged in his shorts, his patience reached its limit. Surveying the room, he found that all of the female members of our clan were present and accounted for. So he figured it was my brother. It was unheard of for a male member to spend more than a few minutes doing his business, except maybe if the meal included refried beans. But this one didn't.

It was then he noticed that his youngest offspring was missing from the room. He knocked on the door, asking his five-year-old son if he was OK. "Yes, uh, fine," my brother answered from behind the door.

"Well, finish up and open the door. There are others waiting to use the bathroom."

"Uhh, I can't. Yet."

"Open the door," he said in that tone we all knew too well. Sergeant Carter barking at Gomer Pyle came to mind.

So he opened the door, and there he stood, holding a cup of water with his tinkler fully submerged.

I don't know what was redder—the crab shells or my little brother's face. "But, Dad! The Old Bay—it burns!"

From that day forward, my mother never had another problem getting him to wash his hands. And life for our little family continued on, crab soup and all.

Uncle Jack showing what a great deal he got on his bottle of gin

Uncle Jack, Mike and Aunt Rita, high school graduation, 1975

# Never Again

by
Mary-Lane Kamberg

Preparing what my family now calls my "World Famous Pineapple Upside-Down Cake That She's Never Making Again" started like most of my culinary adventures. I couldn't open the can of crushed pineapple.

Let's just say I'm not the best cook in my extended family. For group celebrations, I usually bring something I pick up at the deli on the way to the party. That's why I was surprised when my sister Amy, who was planning a family Sunday brunch, asked me to bring the dessert. She knew about my limited gastronomic skill, but she was brave enough to ask me anyway.

A little shocked at her suggestion, I agreed. I love a challenge. This time, I would surprise my family and actually make something, not stop at a bakery.

I called my friend, the one who can cook. "What should I take?" I asked her.

"I have a really easy recipe. It's a pineapple angel food cake.

I'll email it to you."

The evening before the get-together, I went to the store to buy the ingredients. My list included a pre-made angel food cake, a can of crushed pineapple, a package of instant vanilla pudding, a pint of fresh strawberries and an 8-ounce tub of frozen whipped topping. Once home, I unpacked my grocery sack and dug out my mixing bowl from the back of the pantry. I was ready to create.

But as luck would have it, my electric can opener chose that precise moment to go on the fritz. I rummaged through kitchen drawers looking for the manual opener, the one we bought 30 years earlier for a weekend camping trip. It was nowhere to be found.

Even though it was 10 P.M., I ventured next door. Knocking on my neighbor's front door, I shrugged and handed her the can when she answered. She opened the can for me and handed me her old manual opener. "Keep it," she said. I guessed that she and her husband had gone camping once, too.

Back in my kitchen, I followed the recipe, stirring together the pudding mix and crushed pineapple. I emptied the tub of frozen topping into the mixing bowl. Next, I sliced the cake horizontally into two layers and spooned some filling between each layer, and then on the top and sides.

*My friend was right,* I thought. *This is easy.*

But I had a lot of filling left. The recipe said, "Use the remaining filling," so I poured what was left over the top of the cake. The filling seemed a bit runny, but the recipe said to chill the cake before serving. I put it in the refrigerator, expecting the filling to set.

An hour later, I checked on my masterpiece. Then I phoned my friend.

"My cake looks like an erupting volcano a second-grader might make for the science fair. There's filling all over the place," I told her, in near hysterics.

"Tell me what you did," she said, in the tone of a homicide detective looking for clues.

"First, I cut the cake in two."

"You're supposed to have three layers. That would have used the extra filling."

"Even with an extra layer, I'd have lots left."

I read her the steps for the filling and told her I'd mixed together the pudding, pineapple and tub of whipped topping.

"You used the whole tub?"

"It's an 8-ounce tub."

"That's the problem!" my friend said. "You only need one cup."

"Since when does 8 ounces not equal one cup?"

I thought I heard a muffled laugh.

"It's something about dry and liquid measure. You'll have to start over."

So it was back to the 24-hour grocery store for another set of ingredients. Thank goodness I now had my neighbor's can opener! Back home, I went through the steps again, measuring carefully this time. Finally, the second cake was done and topped with a nice ring of strawberries. It looked beautiful.

"Look at the cake!" my sister said the next day when she opened her front door. Amy grabbed the cake plate and headed for the kitchen. "Come out here, everyone. Look at the cake!

Mary-Lane actually made a cake!"

I shook my head, remembering the fiasco of the night before. "I'm never making this again," I told the admiring crowd.

"In that case, I want to take a picture," Amy said. She ran to grab her camera.

In preparation for the photo, I fluffed my hair and primped. When Amy returned, I picked up the cake plate.

Looking through the lens, Amy announced to our family, all of whom had crowded into the kitchen, "This is my sister's dessert that she's never making again!"

I smiled. I was proud of my culinary accomplishment.

But Amy didn't take the photo. She tried to reposition the shot. "I can't quite get the whole cake in the photo," she said to me.

Ever so slightly, I tipped the cake plate forward.

And that is how my beautiful creation became known as the "World Famous Pineapple Upside-Down Cake That She's Never Making Again." It's now a thing of family legend.

Mary-Lane's masterpiece

# Spaghetti Squash

by
Diana M. Amadeo

The small mound of warm vegetarian shreds was topped by savory dabs of sauce. The combined effect caused my mouth to water in delicious anticipation. I had not expected that yesterday's leftovers would be so aromatic and visually appealing, especially while resting on a cheap paper plate. I grabbed my cellphone, lined up the perfect shot and snapped a picture to be distributed nationwide. My accompanying text read: "Spaghetti squash with homemade pesto sauce."

Almost immediately I received a reply message from 3,000 miles away: "Looks wonderful. Tell me your pesto recipe. I have a ton of fresh basil that begs to be eaten."

I smiled at my son's text message. No doubt he had grown his own herbs. His family—his wife and their two young children—had become quite the gardeners. They began planting seeds in the early spring and watched them rise into seedlings under the grow light. Plants emerged to be transplanted to the raised beds in their backyard garden. It did my heart good to know they appreciated fresh veggies. That classic pesto recipe he requested with fresh basil, garlic cloves, pine nuts and shredded Parmesan cheese would most likely be texted to other locations as well.

As I was entering the recipe into my phone, another text popped up. This time from the East Coast: "Looks yummy. Gourmet for lunch? Sigh. Wish I was there."

That quick message was from my daughter, finishing up her studies at MIT. Most of her time was spent in the lab or with her head deeply buried in books. The only time she indulged in fine dining was when her father and I paid a visit to her, taking her out to eat, or when she came home for a visit. She'd come home ready to cook, clean and plant fresh vegetables or flowers.

My cellphone announced another text message, this time from my eldest daughter, the elementary school teacher: "What a coincidence, I have leftover spaghetti squash for lunch, too. Mine is from last night. I baked, shredded and drizzled mine with olive oil, cracked black pepper and grated Parmesan."

*With the help of my three-year-old grandson, probably*, I thought. Cooking is and has always been a family affair.

As in the current menu, we are a family that engages in nutritious downhome cooking and made-from-scratch meals. When my first grandson was born, my husband and I flew to Colorado to meet our precious grandbaby and to help out the new family. It ended up that my son, daughter-in-law and I took turns making healthy meals. When our beautiful granddaughter entered the world, meal planning and baby care in this manner was repeated.

In familiar fashion, my daughter and her husband, who

live locally, share weekend meal plans with us. Their child—grandson #2—has spent a lot of time at Grandpa and Grandmama's house since our daughter returned to work. His soon-to-be-born brother will join him. Every weekday morning, the toddler dons a chef's hat and apron and joins me in the kitchen to whip up some deceptively delicious and nutritious dish. That dish may not involve chocolate chips, but it always involves hugs. Because wherever there is food, there is love.

Growing up with nine siblings, and then having three children and now three grandchildren with another on the way, leaves me with a few baking tricks up my sleeve. Yet, the secrets of teaching children how to eat nutritiously are to be a good example, to let them help in the kitchen and to make food fun and delicious. Many of our family's endearing memories are from the kitchen, as photos adorn our family album: my toddler son covered with flour, my eldest daughter making pizza and my youngest carefully placing strawberries on a fresh fruit salad. There are pictures of our various gardens, too: my son in his OshKosh shorts stealing strawberries out of the patch, my oldest daughter pulling weeds and my youngest doing actual planting. It's good to see these memories continue in my children's families.

My cellphone announces another message. It's from my husband's office: "Lunch looks great. But next time, can we have spaghetti squash the traditional way, you know, with tomato sauce and Italian meatballs?"

I smile inwardly and add his name to my returning text message with the recipe. Then I close my text by typing: "I love you all, Mom."

# Seder Insanity

by
Jamie Krakover

Jewish holidays were always a family affair growing up. Seder is a ritual feast that marks the beginning of Passover. Despite the absence of leavened bread, as in every good Jewish family there was no shortage of food in ours. If you went hungry by the end of the night, you weren't trying hard enough.

For the first Seder, my family gathered at my grandparents' house. Fifteen of us crammed around the dining-room table, all staring at the food as we opened the Haggadah prayer book and started the service.

Two pages in, my cousin whined, "I'm hungry." Unfortunately, the meal didn't come until Page 25 or so. We took turns reading paragraphs, and it wasn't until the next page that someone yelled, "Let's eat!" We all squirmed in our chairs, hungry bellies growling.

At this point, my dad stood at the head of the table and read from the Haggadah as fast as humanly possible. My grandmother and aunt scurried off for the kitchen. We all closed our books despite not finishing and I smiled, ready for food.

My mom waved her finger and said, "But we didn't do the four questions." I huffed and rolled my eyes because as the youngest Hebrew reader, I was stuck with this job. The books flipped back open and I launched into a Hebrew reading of the four questions. It was supposed to be a privilege, but to me, it was the equivalent of being placed in a medieval torture device.

At the conclusion of my broken Hebrew reading, they attempted to make my younger sister read the same passages in English. She always got the easy part and somehow managed to get out of it by batting her eyelashes. My cousin slammed his book down and whined again, "Now can we eat?"

To this my mother replied, "But we forgot to answer the four questions. We can't leave that hanging." The whole room groaned. My grandfather glossed over the few paragraphs, finishing off the answer. Finally, my dad collected the books and the matzo ball soup started appearing.

"One ball or two? Do you want carrots or celery?" my grandmother called from the kitchen, the smell intoxicating us. Every member of the family liked it a different way.

"Two balls and carrots!" I yelled into the kitchen. I hoped my request went to the front of the line to avoid my stomach eating a hole through my abdomen.

The matzo balls were the best part, especially if made correctly, which my grandmother did fabulously light and fluffy. Some families failed at the fine art of crafting matzo balls, making them so hard you could throw them through a wall. Thankfully in my family, the only thing you could crack drywall with was the farfel rolls, a sad attempt at unleavened dinner rolls that I always steered clear of for fear of breaking a tooth.

After dinner came the best part of the evening—the hunt for the Afikoman, otherwise known as dessert. At some point in the service, one of the adults broke the middle matzo, stole away from the service and hid it. The kids' job was to find it, with the prize being $20 from Grandpa.

We jumped up from the table and scrambled around the house, peeking under couch cushions, scanning in plain sight and tripping over each other. After 30 minutes of searching to no avail, I heard my cousin yell from the dining room, "Somebody help me! It's under my dad's ass!"

After bolting to the dining room and watching my cousins wrestle my uncle out of his chair by tickling him, one finally emerged the victor with a giant squashed matzo and the $20 prize. My heart sank because I had failed, once again, to find it. I lined up with the rest of my cousins for the $5 consolation prizes, which was far better than nothing.

As we moved back to the table, no one reached for dessert—at least not the Afikoman. Instead, I sat eating my non ass-warmed strawberries and Passover cake and watched my crazy family, knowing I wouldn't trade them for anything.

# Thanksgiving is Relative

by
Cappy Hall Rearick

Our Thanksgiving began in earnest after the SUV carrying the grandkids from hell was history. Looking at those diminishing taillights was a plentiful reason to give thanks.

My husband, Babe, turned to me. "We survived the kids, but is the house still standing? I can't look." Glancing over his shoulder, I prepared myself for the wreckage.

Our cat Igor lay sprawled on his back with his legs sticking straight up. He had swished his tail so many times I fear he may have broken it. He spent the day hissing, snarling and running from the Jack Russell grandpuppy that chased Igor as though he were covered in Alpo. If he could have, Igor would have begged for Prozac, to which I'd have responded, "Too late." Not too many people know that sucking on Prozac all day instead of hard candy means a quick jumpstart to a Zen experience. Trust me on this.

I didn't decorate for the holiday. Instead, I asked the kids to gather leaves from the yard. They thought up the live frogs on their own. My oldest grandson crafted a groundhog from a brown paper bag and called it a turkey. Not wanting to stunt his possible creative growth spurt, I nodded outwardly and winced inwardly.

Our family barely tolerates the vegetarian who eats nothing that previously wore fur or feathers and the other who eats only Cocoa Puffs. According to my daughter-in-law, she intends to remain on a hunger strike. It will last until she gets the green light to hire a live-in cook. My son, an enthusiastic jug-wine drinker, will eat anything, dead or alive, after a few sips of the grape.

I must have been crazy to think I could restore the ambiance of a traditional sit-down dinner, complete with a Butterball turkey, giblet gravy, dressing made from scratch, yams and football games. Duh.

At 4 P.M., I announced that dinner would be fashionably late. This paved the way for Lucifer's children to entertain everyone by repeating the expletives I had uttered to the Butterball hotline after I discovered my turkey was harder than last year's leftover Halloween candied corn, the same candy I tried to trick this year's trick-or-treaters.

While they gleefully shared videos of my less-than-ladylike behavior taken with their cellphones, I tried to drown them out by playing a tape of my son's bass drum recital at age eight. I was hoping to muffle the sounds of my frozen turkey as it bounced around in the clothes dryer.

Before we sat down for dinner, I suggested, in the spirit of harmony, that the children might like to sit at a separate table.

In a separate room. Next door. I was voted down.

Appreciative onlookers applauding a perfectly carved, golden brown turkey might be a Norman Rockwell sight for some, but it doesn't mean squat to Babe. He doesn't carve; he chops. With that in mind, I thought a discreet turkey-chopping ceremony in the kitchen might be wise. No way did I want anyone to witness him hacking up that turkey as if he were auditioning for the *Saw III* movie.

But when everyone at the table started looking like refugees, my son told his small, unsuspecting children to go in there and whack some speed into their grandfather.

"Stop!" I yelled. "Babe is battling an unarmed turkey with a Ginsu knife. Trust me. This is not something you want your children to see."

My youngest grandson happily chomped his fourth bowl of Cocoa Puffs, making *mmm-mmm* sounds while the rest of us began to rethink cold cereal as a viable alternative to turkey and yams.

It will forever remain a mystery to me why someone would prefer chickpeas to drumsticks, but in deference to the vegan, I had sculpted a small turkey out of tofu using colored toothpicks for the feathers. After brushing it with egg whites, I baked it to a golden glow. When I presented the creation, instead of the appreciation I felt I deserved, I was greeted with howls of laughter and much name-calling. Apparently, positive reinforcement is an easily withheld commodity in my family.

For dessert, I cheated. Instead of the four different desserts I might have made had the turkey thawed like it should have, I popped a Mrs. Paul's pumpkin pie into the oven. When it came out, I put Cool Whip and M&M's on top, the latter addition being another creative surge from the oldest grandson from hell.

There could have been coffee. I can't say for sure because I seized what was left of the wine, closed myself up in a closet and drank that jug dry as Tom Turkey's carcass.

Babe and I have much to be thankful for, but those disappearing taillights? Well, let's just say those taillights took thankfulness to a whole new level.

# CHAPTER FOUR

# What a Trip!

They said it would be memorable.

# Badass
# in the Badlands

by
Melissa Fuoss

Let's face it. Traveling anywhere with your family when you're a 12-year-old girl is straight up embarrassing. Just being in my parents' presence was enough to make me roll my eyes in disgust. I might have survived the family vacation if we were going on a cruise, or to a tropical island, but we weren't. We were headed to the Badlands of South Dakota in our beat-up minivan.

Our vacations invariably began with us backing out of the driveway in the middle of the night. For some inexplicable reason, my parents were crazy enough to think that my slightly younger brother Eric and I would sleep in the car. Instead, the middle-of-the-night car trip made us slap-happy and downright obnoxious. My mother's arm would lengthen in a freaky circus way as she reached all the way to the back seat to slap our knees. "You are going to cause your father to run off the road!" she would yell at us as we suppressed our giggles.

On this particular trip, my brother thought it would be a good idea to eat an entire bag of Rold Gold pretzels. This would not have been a big deal if he would've swallowed them after he chewed them, but he did not. Instead, he spit them out after he got them to just the right consistency and rolled them into a giant chewed pretzel ball. I thought it was ingenious. My parents disagreed.

They were also not impressed when we decided to throw our chewed gum out the window. We probably would've gotten away with it if our van had the cool back windows that rolled down, but this was 1993 and those didn't exist yet—at least not in our world. So imagine sticking a bunch of chewed gum out of the small slit of the pop-out back window. If you are picturing a giant mess of pink goo stuck between the window and the frame of the car, you are right on the money. In order to remedy the situation, my brother and I stuck pens and pencils back there to try to push the gum through. Needless to say, this didn't work and we ended up creating a strange gum/pen/pencil sculpture that prevented the window from closing. The circus arm returned.

Mom would also read to us aloud during these long trips. Somehow she was able to captivate us with novels that we would've never picked out on our own. We heard tales of grasshopper storms and broken families, and as she read, my mind could picture every detail seamlessly. These were the quiet moments of the car trip that I am sure my dad appreciated as he ate sunflower seeds and stared calmly ahead. Eventually, Eric and I drifted off to sleep.

I woke up to the sound of motorcycles. As I sat up and

rubbed my eyes, I thought for sure I was dreaming. There were literally hundreds of motorcycles surrounding us. "What's going on?" I asked as my eyes observed all of the black leather, white fringe and tattoos.

"I'm not sure. They've been like this for the last 30 miles," Dad said while looking in the rear view mirror.

"They're making me nervous," Mom muttered as she closed her book and adjusted her sunglasses.

When it was time to stop for dinner, it was almost impossible to find a restaurant to eat in. There were bikers everywhere, like ants congregating on a melted Popsicle. Eric and I stared with our mouths agape. Many of the women wore tiny white T-shirts that looked as if they were painted on. I had never seen so much leather and denim in my life.

While we ate at the only restaurant that had one remaining open table, we tried to keep conversation about our trip flowing, but it was impossible not to gawk.

One of the bikers passed our table and Dad asked, "Where are all of you guys headed?"

"Sturgis. For the Sturgis Bike Rally this weekend," the biker responded. I am not sure of his name, but if I was placing bets, it was probably "T-Bone." And the tone of his answer was one of, "Duh, how could you not know about the Sturgis Bike Rally?"

Mom promptly gave Dad "the look" and said, "Max, how did you not know this was happening?" Dad shook his head and assured us all would be OK. That's when he said to eat quickly so we could get back on the road to find a motel for the night. With all these people heading in the same direction as we were, finding an available room wasn't going to be easy.

We did find one, though. The sheets were crusty, the bathtub had yellow rings of scum around it and the carpet had a variety of different stains, all varying in texture. We brought our own pillows in and did our best to fall asleep.

Within an hour, the roar of the motorcycles returned, soon followed by sounds of death-metal music blaring at an unnatural volume. The drinking began. And all of the sounds associated with vodka and cheap beer barreled their way through the paper-thin walls into our room.

"Could you keep it down?! There is a family sleeping in here!" Dad yelled as he banged on the wall. No one could hear him. Dad repeated the plea a second time. Nothing.

On his third attempt, he happened to scream it right when there was a pause between songs. "Could you keep it down?! There is a family TRYING TO SLEEP IN HERE!"

"Who the f _ _ k cares?!" was the response.

As the noise level elevated, so did Dad's rage and Mom's anxiety. After an angry debate between my parents, they decided it wasn't safe to keep us here. Hearing more noise, Dad looked through the peephole on the door to discover that the party now involved hundreds of bikers and the chaos had seeped outside the rooms and flowed into the parking lot.

Pointing to a window opposite the parking lot, Dad said, "We're going to have to crawl through the window to get out safely." It was at this moment I actually felt scared. My dad, the big guy who never expressed the emotion of fear, wanted us to crawl out the window to avoid the drunken bikers. This wasn't good.

Mom said she had to take a shower first because the sheets had made her itch. I wanted to tell her that she would never get clean in that bathroom, but I kept my mouth shut. Eric and I began packing our suitcases while Dad figured out how to take the screen off the window. Once the screen was off, Dad hopped out first and Eric and I handed him our luggage. The two of us followed, climbing out the window and fleeing to our getaway van.

And then it happened. While we were waiting anxiously in the van for Mom to crawl out the window, too, we saw the door of our motel room fly open. We watched as she sauntered out of the room and parted the sea of bikers, with her arm up and only her middle finger raised for all to see.

"Holy shit," Dad said in a whisper. Once again, Eric and I were in awe, but this time not at the bikers, but at our mother.

We will never forget that family vacation, and the story has grown in hilarity as time has passed—Mom versus the bikers. And Mom won.

# 36 Ways to Wreck Your Vacation

by
Liane Kupferberg Carter

1. Take your kids.
2. OK. Forget number one.
3. Rent a vacation house from people who don't have kids and don't like kids, the ones who are fond of white, wall-to-wall carpeting, glass sculptures and model ships in bottles.
4. Pull your kid out of camp a week early for your family vacation, thus causing him to miss the end-of-camp carnival. Listen to him cry on your vacation. Promise him that if he stops, you'll get him a digital pet.
5. Listen to Tamagotchi Digital Pet's beeps and wails for hundreds of miles.
6. Forget to bring the carsick bag. Believe your kid has outgrown that problem anyway. Discover you're wrong.
7. Pull off the road and watch your son and husband have a peeing contest.

8. Watch your eight-year-old son win the peeing contest. Endure your husband's muttering about it for the next 100 miles.

9. Listen to your younger child whine, "Mom, he's breathing on me."

10. Listen to the older one ask, "Couldn't we find a nice family to adopt him?"

11. Take along your child's friend who thinks it's hilarious to jam his cheek full of grapes and make gagging noises while you're driving.

12. Arrive to find that when the real estate agent said, "rustic," she meant no indoor plumbing.

13. Call the real estate agent and inquire about maid service. Listen to her cackle.

14. Week One: Unpack those 10 novels you've been dying to read. Week Two: Repack them, all unread.

15. Forget your kid's favorite toy bunny at home. Listen to him sob, "Binky, Binky!" for three nights running.

16. Realize you didn't pack a bathing suit. Have to go buy one. Have to go buy one in the resort boutique where no suit is larger than a size 2 and the dressing room is lit like an airport runway.

17. Let your spouse carry his BlackBerry to the beach. See how well it operates when you get sand in it. See what happens when your toddler drops it later in the pool.

18. Discover it's black fly season. Apply the local bug spray called "Irving's Fly Dope." Discover the dope is Irving— the flies love it.

19. Endure 37 rounds of minigolf with an eight-year-old who cheats.

20. Call home only to hear your mother ask, "And when are we going to see you?"
21. Buy your kid a book of knock-knock jokes to keep him quiet. Be subjected to each one while maintaining a glazed grin.
22. Restrain yourself from slugging your spouse after his hourly query, "Are you relaxed yet?"
23. Be forced to referee your kids' burping contests.
24. Drive by miles of antique shops and craftsmen's galleries without being able to stop and see a single one.
25. Spend 45 minutes sweating while standing in line in a quaint candy store with no air conditioning so you can mail chocolate fudge to all the folks back home.
26. Climb down a steep beach bluff with a toddler on your hip, only to have him immediately need the bathroom located back up top.
27. Offer large cash rewards to the child who can keep quiet the longest.
28. Realize that ice cream is the only source of protein your kids are getting.
29. Arrive at the famous seafood restaurant you've wanted to try. Discover they don't have hamburgers. Let your kids starve.
30. Forget letting your kids starve. Find a hamburger joint.
31. Ask your older child to watch his brother so you can go to the bathroom for two minutes. Return to find your older child's nose pressed to the TV, the front door open and your four-year-old playing in the road.
32. Yell at your older child for letting his brother play in the road. Hear him say, "Well, I only did it once." Hear him ask, "If something happens to him *then* can we get a dog?"

33. Bring the baby sitter on vacation with you. Have no privacy.

34. Don't bring the baby sitter. Have no privacy.

35. Do laundry. Cook. Clean. Sweep sand. Bathe children. Spread suntan lotion. Pack beach toys. Make snacks. Tell yourself it must be a vacation because you've got an ocean view.

36. Finally understand that the phrase "family vacation" is the ultimate oxymoron.

Liane and her two sons at Cape Cod

# The High Lonesome

by
Jerry W. Baker

The High Lonesome was calling. Again!

My brother-in-law Marland and I checked our calendars. We coordinated our schedules for another trip together to the deer lease and were fired up.

The High Lonesome deer lease sprawls across lush, rolling hills in the high country of West Texas. It's 5,000 acres of untouched land that teems with wildlife, wildflowers and wild animals. Whether lease members congregate to hunt or socialize, it's home away from home for guys.

The cabin, fondly referred to as "The Shack," includes all the necessities. It sleeps 10 on lumpy bunk beds positioned against three walls and has a minuscule bathroom with a shower, as well as a tiny kitchen and eating area. Gazing at the ceiling, one is in awe of the ragged insulation hanging in disarray. And there was no heat source inside The Shack.

Deer season in Texas ranks right up there with national

holidays, and good ol' boys prepare for weeks, if not months, in anticipation of opening day during the first week of November. Then in January, doe season begins and the good ol' boys head out again. In that part of Texas, winter weather can be as wretched as anywhere in the country. For this trip, the forecast looked bleak. However, the High Lonesome was calling and Marland and I were going, come hell or high water.

Once we made it to the lease, we unloaded our gear, claimed our bunks and visited with the fellas who had arrived before us. By evening, the two of us were itching to hunt.

The next morning, we headed to the Motel Six. No, not a motel, but a deer stand. Each stand is named, and this one left a lot to one's imagination. While we waited, our teeth chattered, our bones ached and we shivered beneath layers of insulated clothing. Although we never spied one doe, we managed to take out several wild hogs before heading back to The Shack.

Each morning found us positioned in a different deer stand. Some stands were ground level, while others were perched in trees. Marland and I sat in total silence without moving a muscle for hours, and then moaned as we hoisted our frozen bodies into "Bubba Jeep." Yes, vehicles also have names. Back at The Shack, we'd have a hot breakfast.

The evening routine was nearly identical to the morning ritual. However, if the morning hunt brought no luck, a change of stands took place. Some stands are built for two occupants while others are one-man stands. And not all stands are equal when it comes to comfort. Some are not well-built, with wind blasting through cracks and crevices. Others, such as those built by Marland—nicknamed "Master Handyman"—are airtight and constructed to last a lifetime or two. But there's one thing all deer stands lack—a commode!

A few days into the trip, weather conditions improved, although the hunting didn't. On our final evening, Marland dropped me off at a deer stand located 15 feet high in a tree while he headed off to another one. We synced our watches for his return to pick me up. I didn't spot a doe and time passed slowly. Very slowly, in fact, once the stomach cramps hit! And I found myself stuck in the stand!

When Marland finally pulled up, it was nightfall. I frantically waved my flashlight out of the window and yelled, "Where the hell have you been?! I'm locked in this damned thing and I've got to get out—now! Mother Nature is calling!"

Through maniacal laughter, Marland yelled back, "Do you see the white string by the door? Just pull on it! It doesn't require a locksmith to get out of there!"

Spinning around, I spied the idiotic string, gave it a yank and the door popped open. Nearly airborne as I hurried down, I jumped into the Jeep. "Drive fast, Marland! This is no joke!"

My brother-in-law drove like a lunatic over the rocky terrain. Poor old Bubba Jeep clanged and banged like a bucket of nuts and bolts. But I wasn't going to make it.

"Stop this thing, right now! My time is up!"

Once the Jeep lurched to a stop, I launched myself out and headed into scrubby brush. I tossed my heavy coat one way, my lighter jacket another, ready to drop my overalls in a heartbeat. I could hear Marland's laughter even as I distanced myself from him.

Finding a fallen tree, I got down to business. Suddenly, something whizzed past my head so close that I was forced to duck. *What the hell?* I said to myself. Even in the darkness, I saw where it landed, but didn't know what it was. *Is Marland throwing things at me? In my condition?*

"Hey, Jerry! Did you see that?"

"I don't know what *that* was, but you darn near smacked me in the head! Ya think I could have a little privacy? This is no time to be hurling things at me!

"It's just a coffee can."

I heard his guffawing and considered shooting him dead. *Too bad my gun's in Bubba.* That's when I realized I was in dire straits—I had gone into the undergrowth without my gun. Wild hogs were thick, especially after dark, not to mention an occasional mountain lion. And there I sat, exposed and unarmed.

"Hey, Jerry, just relax. I keep a roll of toilet paper in that coffee can so I'm always prepared. Figured you could use it!"

With the emergency now finished, we were back on the road to The Shack. During the drive, I begged Marland not to tell the others about my dilemma. I knew I would never hear the end of it and that hell-raising group of fellas would tease me relentlessly. After miles of bantering, begging and plea bargaining, Marland finally promised to keep his mouth shut.

All seemed well once we rejoined the group. Conversation drifted smoothly from one subject to another. I was convinced that my brother-in-law would stay true to his word.

Upon entering the bathroom to shower, I breathed a huge sigh of relief. But under the soothing, warm water, I heard a deafening explosion of laughter rattle The Shack's rafters. *Damnation! I've been had, and had bad.* Through the paper-thin walls, I heard every wisecrack. I wanted to vanish, but there wasn't even a window to use as an escape route. I'd gone from being locked in a deer stand to being trapped in a john.

Believe it or not, somehow Marland and I remain on speaking terms after that trip. Family is family through thick and thin, even in-laws. And as for those deer-lease hooligans and their passions for nicknames, sure enough I returned home with one—"The High-Lonesome Locksmith!"

Jerry and Bubba

# Closing Time

by
Kendall Roderick

"Attention, customers. We are closing in five minutes."

I run for the door whenever I hear this announcement. Why? Maybe a childhood experience? OK, definitely a childhood experience.

Most people know that castles were built to keep people out. Most of us wouldn't expect castles to keep us in, especially if the "us" is an entire family. However, it is for that very reason I pay attention to closing times.

On a gloomy day in Austria, my family and I were imprisoned, literally stuck behind bars at the top of a mountain in a castle from the ninth century. My mind trailed back to that day and the lady we had seen as we entered.

"Xcuse, xcuse!" she yelled. "Ve cloths soon!"

We were all so exhausted from the climb and excited to see the castle that her warning didn't seem as important at the time. But as I sat with my hands reaching out of the bars of the locked wrought-iron gate, it suddenly became pretty clear to me. In Austria, you don't get five-minute warnings over a loudspeaker. The worst part was that my parents actually acknowledged the lady and her warning as if they understood what she said. Yet they were stuck, just like me.

I could see my dad circling the courtyard, his hand trailing through his hair. "How could they miss us? Four people in a castle and with a baby! Could they really not have seen us?"

*I don't know, Dad,* I said sarcastically to my five-year-old self. There were 108 rooms with only 40 or so open to the public, and if four people could wander around aimlessly without even trying to be quiet, it suddenly made sense to me how all the princesses in movies could so easily escape. *Escape? Yeah, that would be nice. Except those princesses didn't have a bunch of locked gates.*

"They will come back," Mom stated in a matter-of-fact way.

"It's a four-mile hike. You think they just locked all the gates to go on a walk and come back 20 minutes later?" Dad responded. He pushed a hand through his hair again and exhaled. "We might be stuck here all night. We knew we were pushing it when we left late."

"Don't say that," Mom screeched. "We can't be stuck here with the baby."

"It isn't like we have a choice. Saying it out loud doesn't make it more true than not saying it at all."

I wiggled my fingers as I continued to watch my hands outside of the bars. If only all of me were as tiny. Sure, my five-month-old sister could have fit through, but how could a baby help? For this reason, I didn't bother mentioning my escape plan to my parents.

A sign dangled on the gate a few feet above me. It looked as if it said, "Ve Cloths," but I didn't say anything about that either. It wasn't like I could read broken English, anyway.

Thunder cracked in the distance. It had rained earlier on the way up to the castle. I wondered what we would do—hide in the castle to find shelter from the rain and possibly miss anyone who returned? I looked up at the clouds moving in above us.

"Help!" I looked behind me to see my mother yelling into the air. "Someone help us! We are trapped in this castle!"

It was always amusing when someone yelled a full sentence. I giggled.

"Kendall, help me."

My smile vanished. So much for the giggle. It got me roped in.

"Help!" I yelled, as I grabbed onto the bars of the gate. I felt powerful, "Help!" I screamed.

"Louder, Kendall. You, too, honey," Mom said to Dad.

"Help!" Dad yelled and soon we became a chorus. My little sister joined in by wailing. It's the family music you normally only hear on the holidays. I covered my ears and screamed louder.

"Wait," Dad said. We all went silent. "I think I see someone." He ran to the gate where I sat. "Kendall, do you see him? Wave."

I waved my small hands.

"We're in here!" Dad yelled to a small speck in the distance.

I watched as the speck got larger and soon became a complete person. It took some time before he got to us. Dad picked me up from the gate as the man got out his keys.

"Ohhh, boy! Is goot I hat hurt something, unt kum see

vut is. Yu vood have ben looked up the ole night," the man chuckled. "I hat thinked all hat gone a vile bak. So I lock." He laughed again.

I couldn't understand a word, but watched as my parents continued the conversation until we were freed.

So that's why, as an adult, I pay attention to the time. I certainly never hesitate to run for the doors when a voice from speakers blares above my head, "Closing time!"

Especially if I'm with my family.

Kendall with her parents and baby sister outside the infamous castle

# The Last Camping Trip

by
David Martin

My father was an enigma. Not one of those enigmas wrapped in a mystery locked inside a puzzle. He was an ordinary, run-of-the-mill enigma, but an enigma nonetheless.

From outward appearances, my dad would pass as a card-carrying member of the proletariat. His full head of unkempt black hair, together with his complete disregard for fashion, announced to the world that here was a man who undoubtedly worked with his hands. And when he spoke to people in his unpretentious, down-to-earth manner, it was clear that whatever my dad did for a living, it involved more physical than mental labor. But my dad did not work with his hands. Despite growing up in poverty, he somehow managed to acquire a Ph.D. and a career as a physics professor at a small northern New York engineering school.

My father didn't start out as a handyman. After a full day of teaching physics to seldom-interested students and dealing with the irrational demands of college administrators, he needed a hobby where he could pound, hammer and cut until his daily frustrations evaporated into a flurry of physical activity. Living in a huge, drafty 100-year-old house automatically created an ongoing legion of handyman chores. Since money did not—as my father frequently reminded us four kids—grow on trees, he was forced by circumstances to learn how to do everything from plumbing to roof repairs himself. Eventually, Dad graduated to actual construction. Over time, in an ad hoc fashion, he even managed to create his own workshop in the dank, dark cellar beneath our antebellum home, complete with workbench and table saw.

So it perhaps should not have surprised me that one of his early 1960s projects was a camper trailer built to help launch our family into a new era of communal vacationing. For years, our holidays had primarily consisted of packing the whole family into whichever of our secondhand cars had the best chance of making it and driving thousands of miles east or west to spend time with relatives. Apart from the occasional day at a local beach, no one, to my recollection, had suggested we get in touch with nature. So the trailer came as a surprise to all of us.

With the advantage of hindsight, I can see now that it was an unfortunate meeting of minds that took us on this new adventure. Mom wanted us to "try camping." Since Dad wasn't a camper, Mom's desire might have lain dormant for years. But since he was now a bona fide builder of things, he approached her wish as a new handyman challenge. The result was a family camper which was unique in design and execution. It consisted of a gray-painted plywood contraption that fit inside a two-wheeled trailer of the type more commonly used to haul rocks, bricks or sand.

So late that June, our family headed for our little piece of Eden in the Adirondack Mountains, a place called "Schroon Lake." Or as every 12-year-old boy, including me, cleverly named it—"Screwin' Lake."

The first day was ideal: mid-70s, sunny—a perfect portent of a perfect camping weekend. And when we finally arrived at Schroon Lake, it seemed as if our luck couldn't get any better. Considering summer had officially begun and it was a Friday afternoon, there was hardly anyone else at the lakeside campground. We couldn't believe our good fortune—we had our pick of sites. Mother Nature was surely smiling on us.

There was a reason, however, why the campground was nearly deserted and why prime, lakeside venues were there for the taking. Anyone with any sense was at home snug in their beds. For it was black-fly season.

As the sun set, we began to get a harbinger of the night ahead of us. Tiny little bugs congregated around our heads. But we figured it wasn't a big deal—we would simply retire to our marvelous new camper and wait out the bugs until morning.

We were wrong. There were no defenses on the camper against the tiny flies. The screen on the back door had a mesh designed to bar squirrels and possibly overgrown houseflies, but not black flies. Anything smaller was free to come and go as it pleased.

With all six of us squished into the camper, we began to

experience an hours-long symphony comprised of squishing air mattresses, slapping hands, crying children and the occasional, "Goddamit, Jean, whose idea was this?" from Dad. One by one, we exited the camper in search of relief.

Hours later, the sun mercifully rose and the black flies abated. Bloodied and decidedly bowed, we quickly gave up. No one suggested we stay and wait things out, not even my mother. I don't recall another family camping trip—ever. In fact, I don't recall anyone in my family ever willingly undertaking another getaway into the great outdoors.

As for the camper, once we got home, it was removed from the trailer and placed in the side yard. Once it became clear that the camper would never be used again, Dad dismantled it and used the gray plywood for other, much safer handyman projects—like the plywood boat that wouldn't float. But that's another family story for another day.

The Martin family, with David sitting on the far right

# The Witches of Yellowstone

by
Kathe Campbell

Witches have fascinated and horrified many in our culture for centuries. For example, one can't forget Shakespeare's three witches brooding over a bubbling cauldron in *Macbeth* and chanting, "Fire burn and cauldron bubble." And what about *The Wizard of Oz's* Wicked Witch of the West, her face green and haggard and her pointy hat trailing a black veil? This famous witch flew across the pages of books, movie screens and eventually TV sets on her broomstick, cackling and shrieking her terrifying threats to all those in Oz, including the heroine Dorothy and her little dog Toto. Today, witches of all shapes and sizes are alive and well, from books to movies to TV shows and even on the streets of our nation during Halloween trick-or-treating.

When our young family was growing up, Katie, our four-year-old, found an old copy of *The Wizard of Oz* and begged me to read it to her and her older sister Molly. Written by Frank Baum, the book Katie had found had been my mother's.

With its scuffed cover and crimped pages, the book brought back so many childhood memories. I was tickled my little ones had asked me to read it aloud to them before bedtime.

"Sounds like fun, but only a chapter or two each night," I happily answered. "Molly, jump in beside Katie. Lights out by 9:30."

Every evening for several days, both girls sat mesmerized as I animated the words with dramatic flair, allowing my voice to drop and soften in all the right places. The munchkin's high-pitched monotones kept the girls in stitches, as did my impression of the wailing and screeching witch. My acting was so dramatic that come early morning, I had to suck on throat drops after voicing the entire cast, including the Wizard and Dorothy's assortment of tag-along compatriots.

On Easter Sunday, one of the major television networks touted the showing of *The Wizard of Oz*. Our whole family looked forward to the broadcast and we made lots of popcorn for the special event. Watching the opening scenes made me think back to a wondrous time when my own parents took me to see the popular film when it first opened in theaters back in the Dark Ages. Now, with my children and husband, I sat enthralled again, glued to each familiar character, wrapped in the arms of nostalgia I hoped to never forget.

Our kids—son Tim and Katie and Molly—loved the movie. My poor husband somehow missed seeing the movie when it first came out, his family no doubt unable to cough up the change in the throes of the nation's ghastly Depression. As a family, we viewed every electrifying scene together, enrapt and full of emotion, with the children sprawled on the floor adding their own brand of sound effects. I was glad we girls had read the book together that winter.

Summer brought on pure déjà vu during a family trip to Yellowstone Park. Tim, Katie and Molly toured the thermal water features together. Six years older, Tim held his sisters' hands tightly, reading the signs aloud as they traveled along the terraces and boardwalks. The three stood paralyzed as the geysers unleashed whooshing, scalding reservoirs gushing skyward then slowly died, leaving rushing rivulets in their wake.

As the boiling aqua hot pools, fumaroles and mud pots spat and steamed, Tim delivered a bewitching incantation by chanting legendary toils and troubles. Not to be outdone, Molly and Katie mimicked the fun as fellow sightseers giggled at their *Oz* antics. Surprised over their reactions, Katie screeched, "Did you folks see the movie, too?"

Continuing their walk, the kids came upon another mud pot. "Look here at this, you guys," grinned Tim, "all that yucky, smelly, rotten egg stuff is what the mean old Wicked Witch of the West stirs in her cauldron."

"Oh, Timmy, there are no rotten eggs in *The Wizard of Oz*," Molly said, dampening his fun. But four-year-old Katie believed Tim's satirical joshing.

The day had been long and we had reservations for dinner that night at the Old Faithful Lodge. Before we entered the lodge, we waited for the renowned Old Faithful Geyser to rumble and spurt, spewing her historic surges of boiling water 145 feet into the air. Tourists, cameras and camcorders were poised and ready, everyone talking excitedly up and down the decked concourse.

Suddenly Katie spied a group of habited nuns sightseeing

along the boardwalk. She yanked on Tim's hand and shrieked in deafening curiosity, "What are those witches doing here, Timmy?"

Tim motioned for her to shush, Molly muzzled her mouth, their father brandished an irritable grin and I wanted to die from humiliation. Uproarious laughter emanated from what seemed to be more than 1,000 onlookers. And my consternation turned to utter relief when the nuns stopped and chuckled politely at our precocious child.

"Katie," scolded Tim after the nuns had left, "those are not witches. They are the ladies from the Catholic Church. You've seen nuns before."

"No, I haven't, Timmy," Katie resounded. "I've never seen nuns all dressed up like witches before. They must be the good witches from the north, because they have such nice faces."

We stood there as a family, smiling over our youngest daughter's candid observation. Then we laughed again when Katie added, "Next Halloween, I want to dress up as a good witch, just like them!"

Yellowstone
National Park's
Old Faithful

# The Grand Pause

by

## Dahlynn McKowen

There are some moments in life that stay with you forever. One such moment happened to me during a 1976 summer family vacation.

Our destination was North Dakota, where my dad's family lived. He was born and raised there on his family's farm. The six of us—Mom, Dad, three younger siblings and myself—would make the trip from our home in California to North Dakota in our old station wagon.

As part of our trip, Mom insisted on stopping in Utah for a few days to visit her family. She also insisted on making stops here and there so we kids could escape the car and run off some energy. Dad never liked to stop for anything—once he got behind the wheel, he would drive straight through. If he had his way, Dad would have driven night and day to make North Dakota in record time, regardless if we needed to stop to stretch or eat or even pee. But he gave in to Mom's insistence to make frequent stops, which was a good thing—holding my bladder for hours on end would have been a challenge.

With the car packed to the brim inside and piled high on top with everything a family of six needed, including camping equipment since staying in a hotel was a luxury, we set off, crossing the Sierra Nevada into the vast desert that covers much of the state of Nevada. Thankfully it wasn't too hot yet. Back in those days, air conditioning in cars was another luxury we couldn't afford, so we kept the car windows rolled halfway down to let the air in and keep the bugs out.

During our trip, Mom planned on entertaining us with car games such as "I Spy" and the license plate challenge, where the first one to call out a license plate from every state would win a prize. But the Nevada desert was unforgiving—there wasn't much to spy and very few cars traveled the empty interstate. Bored to tears and driving both our parents nuts, Mom finally gave us rambunctious souls a treat—Dramamine. The reason it was a treat was because we got to wash the pills down with Kool-Aid, one of our favorite drinks.

Needless to say, when evening came on the first day of our grand adventure, we kids weren't very helpful erecting the tent. We were too tired and groggy from the car-sick medicine. But since I was the eldest—age 16—I was quickly put to work holding tent posts while Dad hammered in the stakes and tied on the ropes. Remember, this was back in the days when tents didn't pop together like the lightweight tents of today. These were the days of non-collapsible, one-piece tent poles, very heavy canvas fabric and driving stakes into the ground and tying off the poles with thick rope. It was considered a miracle if we got the tent up in under an hour.

After breakfast the next morning, we packed up camp and headed across the Great Salt Lake. That night, we would stay with a relative just south of Salt Lake City. For this reason, Mom didn't give us any Dramamine—she wanted her darling children awake and alert, not falling asleep at our host's dinner table that evening.

After crossing the white vastness of the Great Salt Lake, Mom decided it would be a good idea to stop at Temple Square. Located in downtown Salt Lake City, the 10-acre Temple Square is the Mecca of Latter-day Saints and home of the Mormon religion. It had been years since Mom had been there, and Dad and we kids had never seen the place. The idea was to let us four kids explore the grounds and burn off some pent-up energy before heading to our relative's home.

Dad found a parking space for the family wagon. After unloading and primping so we would be presentable, we all made our way into Temple Square. We were allowed to run—politely, of course—around the beautiful grounds. We looked at nearly everything and were disappointed we couldn't go inside the actual temple—since we weren't Mormon, we weren't allowed in.

After an hour, the four of us were tired and wanted to sit down and rest. That's when Mom had another idea—the family could attend a scheduled music recital in the famed Tabernacle. Itching to get back on the road, Dad wasn't thrilled, but he agreed.

Entering the grand hall, we quickly found seats about 15 pews back from the front. We all stared up at the huge pipe organ, the one we had seen on television. As a kid, everything always appears bigger. And that was especially true in this case—the great organ, considered back then to be one of the world's largest musical instruments, towered above us. We were in awe.

Suddenly, music blasted out of the monstrosity, making us jump. No one could be seen playing the organ, which bored my siblings and me very quickly. But wanting to please Mom, and also worn out from running around, we sat like good children in church. The organ droned on and on, playing hymns and famous works of music. The music hall was packed with tourists and worshippers. Some people sang along when a hymn played, while others listened intently.

As the monotonous recital drew to a close, the music became more intense. Catching our attention, the four of us scooted to the edge of our pew, excited at the prospects that the concert was almost over. The pipe organ sang like crazy then stopped for a few seconds before hitting its final, grandiose note. And it was during those few seconds of silence that the unthinkable happened.

Dad snored. Not just his normal "I'm-napping" snore, but a booming, foghorn snore. We kids had no idea he had fallen asleep.

Mom was mortified. She quickly stared at us, warning us with her eyes not to laugh. But unable to contain our giggles, we laughed aloud, right along with the other recital goers. Startled awake by the burst of laughter—which drowned out the final notes of the recital—Dad was more startled by Mom's glare. Needless to say, it was a very quiet ride to our relative's home.

For the rest of the 3,000-mile, three-week family trip, every time we saw a church, we asked Dad if he wanted to stop and take a nap. True to form, he kept right on going.

Dahlynn (far right) with her parents and younger siblings, 1976

The family station wagon, loaded and ready to go on vacation

# CHAPTER FIVE

# Oh, Crap!

The nitty-gritty truth of the matter.

# Home Movies

by
Laurel McHargue

Some things you simply cannot unsee. For example, personalities in our world of reality TV are accustomed to warning viewers when such a "thing" is about to accost potentially delicate sensibilities.

It's nice to be offered the opportunity to turn away or to peer, feigning revulsion, through fingertips. I remember how Grandma used to avert her eyes from her soap opera, clucking in disgust when the horny young actors would lock lips. I was always pretty sure that her peripheral vision didn't miss a lick, but she could not allow herself the Peeping-Tom pleasure of blatant viewing with young grandchildren waiting expectantly for a channel change. Thinking back on this, oh, how I wish I could have saved my young brother-in-law and his new wife that one fateful afternoon from the visual I can only pray they will someday forget.

Being a good mother to my perfect first-born child, Nick,

I never missed an opportunity to capture his brilliance on videotape. From Nick being born—filmed from an artfully discreet angle—until years later when he had to share the limelight with his little brother, Nick was the center of my universe. And it was always my pleasure to immortalize him on film.

Being a good wife to my husband, who was patient during those early years when his spotlight had been stolen by a drooling, farting, adorably dependent little upstart, I did what I could to keep our own flame alive—or at least smoldering. The difficulty of this challenge would increase significantly when military orders separated us for several months. But aha! We owned a camcorder with a tripod, and I had several sets of sexy lingerie stashed away. I put them all to use to create a very special, very naughty home movie to mail to my husband for Valentine's Day. After receiving the tape, he called me, and that call left me tingling with anticipation of our reunion the following month.

Having returned to our senses and sensibilities once we were together again, we both agreed that my X-rated video had no place on the shelf with *Aladdin* and *Peter Pan*. We would do the responsible thing and record over the risqué scenes with more family-friendly footage. I was relieved to know that my life as a soft-porn film star would never be exposed on *60 Minutes*.

Nope! Not on *60 Minutes,* which I was probably watching with my visiting in-laws when I suggested that it was time to view some family videos. They hadn't been around to witness their nephew's every waking moment, and I secretly wanted to send them home with thoughts of perhaps creating their own little cherub.

I removed the tape from the camcorder and slipped it into the VCR. There was Nick, messy-faced with breakfast goop. There was Nick, pulling himself up at the edge of the couch. There he was again, taking his first unsteady steps . . . snuggling with his stuffed tiger . . . giggling from belly tickles . . . sitting in a large cardboard box. What an adorable child! We laughed together at his antics and Nick laughed with us as he played with his toys on the floor, looking as cute as ever.

Suddenly, without warning and in the middle of another adorable moment, there was . . . ME! And not me, the doting mommy!

Shocked, it took far too long for the scene we were all watching to register in my maternal brain. When it finally did, I let out an involuntary scream and threw my body across the TV screen, desperately seeking the "off" button. My outburst and bizarre behavior frightened my little child, who began to cry.

With the television off, I swept Nick into my arms, but not before registering the expressions on the faces of the innocent young couple I would share holidays with for the rest of my life. Confused and embarrassed, but still staring at the screen, the two of them sat stone-like, eyes wide-open, jaws dropped.

I honestly cannot remember what I blabbered once I quieted my child and could once again see straight. The heat from my face probably contributed to our current global-warming situation. I do remember nervous laughter and apologies. *Perhaps my lightning-fast reflexes thwarted their ability to really see much?* I secretly wondered. But I knew the answer, and it was, "No."

The damage was done. They had both seen what they might never be able to unsee, and the thoughts I sent them home with after that unforgettable visit likely had nothing to do with making babies. Although we never, ever talked about "the incident" again, I also never again suggested to anyone in the family that it was time to watch home movies

Come to think of it, I should probably find out where those old recordings are packed away . . . just in case.

Nick

# I Should
# Have Listened

by
Christine Cacciatore

When I was young, I loved to be scared. I would plead with my parents to scare me, as I loved the feeling. They would occasionally oblige my requests—one time, my mother startled me by jumping out of a closet, which scarred me forever. And I loved it.

But I suppose that you live and learn. I was only 11 years old when the story I'm about to share occurred. That's when I realized I still had a lot to learn.

One evening, my parents rented the movie *Trilogy of Terror*. They told me I couldn't watch it, but I hid behind the couch and watched it anyway.

I should have listened to my parents. It was the scariest movie I had ever seen up to that point in my young, movie-watching life. "Trilogy" means three of something, which is hilarious because I have no memory at all of what the other two horror stories were about. That's because nothing could be scarier than the first story in the movie, the one about a small wooden warrior doll that comes to life.

The story was about a woman who bought a 12-inch-tall African tribal doll to give as a gift to her boyfriend. The doll had countless jagged teeth, held a very sharp spear and wore a little gold chain around his waist. The note that came with the doll said that if the chain ever fell off, an evil demon would possess the doll and bring it to life.

The woman, who was at home alone, went down the hall-way to draw a bath. Moments later, the chain fell off the doll! The evil doll, with those big sharp teeth, immediately came to life and he wanted to stab the woman with his little spear! The possessed doll was so scary to me—he could have easily been Freddy Krueger and Pinocchio's love child. I know that's not possible because Freddy and Pinocchio are both guys, but remember, I was young. And the sound this doll made as it chased the woman around the house was horrifying.

For me, the aftermath of this movie was, at best, unpleas-ant. Everything about it frightened me so badly that even the smallest sound that evening made me jump. When this happened, I found it hard to form words because my mouth wouldn't work. And I couldn't get warm when I was snuggled deep under the covers on my bed. I was petrified.

I should have listened.

That night, and for many nights afterward, I dreamed about that tribal doll. I couldn't avoid dreaming about it. In my night-mares, the little wooden man chased me or surprised me by jump-ing out from behind a curtain or a closed door. Or, heaven forbid, he would slowly crawl up underneath my covers—like an Army soldier does when prone on the ground—as I slept. With a spear in his teeth. To kill me.

My parents didn't help matters any. They found out I had watched the movie and knew how bad it had scared me. True to form, they used that knowledge to their benefit. They reveled in scaring me. It seemed like a contest between the two, to see who could scare me more.

Shortly after viewing the horror movie from hell, Dad, who was a policeman, drove his police cruiser past me while I was walking to school. He rolled down the window and told me in a creepy voice that he had a "special friend" in the car with him who wanted to say, "Hi." I knew what that meant—the little evil doll had gotten to him! I was terrified and ran the rest of the way to school, but could still hear my dad laughing as he pulled away.

My mother waited until my back was turned then drummed on the table, which sounded like tiny footsteps were running for me. That sound filled me with panic.

In short, my parents—in good fun, of course—preyed on my terror.

The crescendo came one night while I was innocently soaking in the tub in our upstairs bathroom, blissfully unaware that my parents were planning something big . . . a unique and creative prank just for me.

I stopped splashing when I heard a noise come from down the hall. I leaned up out of the tub, which was close to the door, slowly opened the door and peeked out into the hallway. I saw nothing—the coast was clear.

*Well, that was weird*, I thought. I settled back down into

the tub. Then I heard another noise, several bumps then a rhythmic *ree-ree-ree* sound.

My blood went cold and my heart began to spasm. My hands shook as I pushed the door open again a tiny bit. I expected to see nothing. I hoped to see nothing. However, it was there, in the hallway. It jerked down the hall, toward the bathroom, where I was naked and defenseless in the bathtub. It was holding a spear.

The noise it made was terrifying. Bathwater wasn't the only thing in the tub at that point, unfortunately.

*Ree. Thump. Ree. Thump. Ree. Thump.*

It would have been nice to see what was coming down the hall to get me, but I was not wearing my glasses. The only thing I could make out was that whatever was coming my way was little, had the ability to walk and was carrying a weapon.

That was all I needed to spur me into action.

I jumped out of the tub, grabbed a towel, flung it around me and flew out of the bathroom in the other direction to my room, screeching the entire time. Once inside my room, I hastily grabbed my glasses off the dresser and jammed them onto my face. Then I peered out into the hall.

I should have known. There was my mother, on the floor in the hallway, convulsing with laughter. And with clearer vision—thanks to my glasses—I saw that the horrible African tribal doll with the pointy teeth was actually a smiling, walking babydoll armed with a nut pick.

Her prank was brilliant. Looking back on this and other various dirty tricks my parents played on me while I was growing up, it's a wonder that now, as an adult, I appear to be normal.

I have never stopped watching scary movies, though, and as horrible as it is to admit, I have followed in my parents' footsteps. The lessons I learned from them have served me well. I have scared the heck out of my children, and I'm confident they'll pass this along to their children. The fear and joy of being scared may stretch for generations to come.

I'm off to hide behind the door now. My daughter's due home any minute, and I want to be there to welcome her.

# The Toupee

by
### John Reas

Male-pattern baldness had been a genetic trait on both my mother's and father's side of the family as long as I could remember. How my family approached the possibility of becoming follicle-challenged was as much a reflection of the fashion and societal norms of the times as it was personal taste.

On one hand, my mom's father enjoyed looking like the actor Telly Savalas of *Kojak* fame, and he dutifully shaved his scalp to a nice sheen. While my sister would be mortified at the many times our maternal grandfather would take a napkin when sitting with us in a restaurant and swipe his head as if he were polishing a bowling ball, I thought he was being the epitome of looking cool, like Yul Brynner.

On the other hand, my dad's dad would carefully comb his wispy locks every day to give the resemblance of having a full head of hair, which unfortunately was never quite successful on a windy afternoon. Still, a head of hair was considered an important part of one's appearance, and by the 1970s, the long, unkempt hair that men had worn a decade earlier had evolved into a stylish combination of mullets, shag cuts and comb-overs that all of us had adopted. The "chrome-dome" look was simply no longer acceptable.

This new look was something my dad was only too aware of, and even though he would carefully comb his hair to give the appearance of having a decent cover, there was no escaping the fact that he was fighting a losing battle in the gene pool. As he kept up with men's fashion during the 1970s and changed his wardrobe to accommodate wide ties and three-piece suits, he also did his best to style his hair and hide his receding hairline—that is until he decided it was time to invest in a toupee.

I was in sixth grade back then. When Dad came home one Saturday afternoon with his new hairpiece, I was shooting hoops in the driveway. He stepped out of our big family Buick and I did a double take, missing the basket. Instead of a thin layer of graying hair, he had a distinguished salt-and-pepper mane that was carefully groomed and styled. It was an amazing transformation, and I couldn't help but exclaim, "Wow, Dad! That's a heck of a look! What's it made out of? Is it real fur? It looks like something Jeremiah Johnson would have worn." I had received a Davy Crockett hat made from real raccoon skin for Christmas and thought anything made from animal skins was boss.

Dad looked at me, sighed and shook his head, "No, it's not made out of animal fur. It's synthetic. So, what do you think? I want to go in and surprise Mother. I think she'll really like it."

Trying for a layup, I answered, "Well, I'm sure she'll be

surprised. You're looking different and all. But, it's definitely cool looking."

Dad beamed and walked into the house.

A moment later, through the kitchen window, I could hear Mom shriek, followed by the clattering of plates. "Who are you?!" she said. Then a moment later, she followed with, "Oh, dear, I didn't recognize you at first!"

Yep, Dad had succeeded in surprising Mom.

Over the next few weeks, our neighbors and friends became acquainted with Dad's new appearance, and the reviews were positive. Not only did his toupee fit well, but it added a look of stature that had been diminishing with the receding hairline. Before he left for work in the morning, he would painstakingly apply adhesive to his shaved scalp and place his hairpiece on so that it seamlessly blended with his overall appearance. The ritual could take up to 30 minutes in the morning, but there was no doubt that Dad looked and felt great, and was ready to conquer the world every day once his preparations were completed. Overnight, he became 10 years younger, and that quickly became evident the following week when we were at our neighbor's house for a barbecue.

The Martins were the only ones in the neighborhood who owned a swimming pool, and every year around the Fourth of July, they would invite us over for a barbecue and pool party. It was always a great time with the Martin kids, who were similar to us in age. And following an afternoon of hot dogs, hamburgers and watermelon, we all would go downtown to the riverfront for the annual city fireworks display.

But that afternoon, as we were splashing about in the

pool, I noticed Dad by the grill talking to Old Man Martin. Both of them were laughing about something, and then Dad looked over to where a bunch of us played chicken in the pool. I watched him set down his burger and beer and peel off his shirt. He had worn his swimming trunks to the party, but none of us figured he would actually go into the pool while we were there.

We were wrong. He took a mighty jump off the side of the pool, curled up his legs and wrapped his arms around his knees then cannonballed into the water with a huge splash. All of us cheered as the tsunami swept over us, and then Keith Martin shouted, "Hey, there's a squirrel in the pool!"

I looked over and saw a furry-looking object floating on the surface as Dad bobbed to the top, wiped the water from his face, and then reached for the top of his head. His eyes grew wide as he touched his bare scalp. That's when he noticed his toupee floating nearby. He reached over, grabbed it and slapped it on his head. He quickly grabbed the pool ladder and pulled himself out of the water. Mr. Martin was grinning, but Dad was scowling as he toweled himself dry. It didn't help matters that Dad had accidently placed the toupee on backward.

We kids just shrugged at each other, but Keith yelled, "Hey, Mr. R, did you know your toupee kind of looks like an otter in the water?" We all laughed. "And that was a great cannonball! Can you do it again? Man, that was a great tidal wave! Kind of like in *The Poseidon Adventure*."

Dad simply replied, "Glad you liked the waves, kids. I think I'll pass on the pool. Just had a big meal and all, you know."

Dad readjusted his toupee as best as he could then took off for the house. Later, both of our families went to the riverfront to watch the fireworks. By then, Dad's top was dried, combed and firmly back in place. We met up with the Martins there and set out our blankets and lawn chairs, while Mr. Martin pulled out several packages of sparklers for the kids to play with. No one commented about the pool incident, but I couldn't help noticing as the night sky erupted with crimson, blue and white that Dad kept tapping his head, reassuring himself that his toupee was still in place.

After that, Dad was determined his toupee would remain fixed in place regardless of the conditions he encountered. He had been assured by the store where he purchased the toupee that the adhesive he was using would keep his hairpiece in place, regardless of how wet and windy it was outside. Dad became more diligent in the morning, carefully applying the toupee's solution to his scalp. Soon, the incident at the pool was behind him, and we all got used to seeing him in the morning with the new look when we had breakfast.

But it didn't last long. One Sunday morning in August, we were all getting ready for church. Outside, a torrential storm had blown in.

"Come on, it's getting late," Dad said from the foot of the stairs. Mom and the rest of us trooped down in our Sunday best. He added, "Remember, we're having brunch with Grandpa after church."

"Can we have pizza?" I asked.

"No, you know he likes that cafeteria on Sylvania. We'll take him there."

I was crestfallen. *Old people food*, I sadly thought to myself. I was hoping that with his new top, Dad would have adjusted the family menu, as well. Unfortunately, the younger appearance hadn't changed the usual Sunday drill when it came to dinner with our relatives.

We all piled into the Buick, which was parked in the garage. Dad opened the garage door by hand—we didn't have an automatic opener.

"Look at that wind!" he exclaimed when he jumped inside to back the car out. He stopped in the driveway and turned to Mom. "Honey, let me borrow the umbrella while I close the garage door."

He stepped outside and popped open the umbrella. Just then, a huge gust of wind blew by, turning it inside out. Dad was hanging on with one hand as he fumbled with the other, trying to pull the umbrella back in; the more he struggled, the wetter he got and we could hear him cursing as he fought the elements. Finally, he managed to get it closed and quickly reached overhead to close the garage door. At that critical moment another strong gust of wind came over him, and in a flash, it ripped his toupee off his head and discarded it in a puddle of standing water in the grass next to the driveway.

All of us were staring out the window as Dad let out a resounding four-letter word that wasn't one we expected on the way to church. He was furious as he grabbed the soaking-wet hairpiece that looked suspiciously like a drowned rat, yanked open the back door of the Buick and threw it in where it landed on the floor between my brother and me.

The two of us could barely hold our laughter. Mom turned

around in her seat, her eyes twinkling, and said, "Now boys, not a word. NOT A WORD! You hear me?"

I muttered, "Yes, ma'am," as Dad finished closing the garage door, stomped to the Buick and got in.

"Stupid toupee! What a rip-off. I'm putting on the adhesive and letting the hair sit in place for the proper amount of time, and it still blows off with the first windstorm. I should just give up."

"Now, dear, it was a freak occurrence. I'm sure this won't happen again," Mom said. She was always good at reassuring all of us, and she knew just how much the toupee meant to Dad.

"I'm sure you're right. Boys, just leave the toupee there and I'll pick it up when we get home."

He put the car into reverse and started to back out of the driveway when my younger brother blurted out, "Oh, yuck! What is that?"

I looked down at the toupee and saw what my brother was pointing at. There was a brown smear covering half of the hairpiece, and it didn't look like mud. I wrinkled my nose and answered, "Dog poop."

The Buick jolted to a stop. Dad looked back at us. "What?"

We both pointed at the culprit. Mom said, "Well, I do smell something. But, let's just go. We'll be late."

Dad put the car in park, opened the door, got out and opened the back. Reaching over us, he gingerly picked up the toupee and walked it to the garbage can. He dropped the hairpiece into the can and the lid clanged as he slammed it back in place.

Without another word, Dad got back behind the wheel and we left for church, arriving just as the pastor was extending his greeting.

That afternoon, when we arrived home after brunch with Grandpa, Dad decided to go the Telly Savalas route. Thankfully, he never sucked on lollipops or asked, "Who loves ya, baby?"

John's dad (left) sporting his toupee

# Crazy Old Saint

by
Bobby Barbara Smith

"Who you looking for?!" a neighbor called out as I was knocking on my aunt's door.

Before I could answer, she continued with her diatribe. "She's not there. She left early. She's probably out going through people's trash. Are you from Social Services? Someone needs to do something about her. She's crazy!"

I breathed deeply. "Thank you," I replied, with a cold stare and a forced smile. I wanted to say more, but knew that to some degree the neighbor was speaking the truth.

We all have family members whose behavior is edgy and questionable. In our family, it was my dad's sister—my name-sake—Aunt Jean. I don't know how Dad snuck that past Mom. Aunt Jean was everything mother despised. Mother tried to keep me away from her, but there were times when even her best efforts failed.

Aunt Jean would show up on our doorstep with a different

boyfriend and boxes of old clothing each time—a gift for our family. Mother would scrub the clothing as if the devil himself were attached, and then rework the fabric to make what she called "suitable clothing."

One box had the most beautiful sheer blue panties. My panties were all plain-Jane white cotton. I had no idea something like this existed! "Mom, they're beautiful! Please, may I keep them?"

Mom held them at arm's length, clicking her tongue in disapproval. "Let me see what I can do." And with that, she disappeared into the bedroom.

Listening to her sewing machine clacking away behind the closed door, I wondered what she meant. She emerged with a smug look of satisfaction and handed me the panties. She had lined my delicate panties with heavy white cotton!

One Christmas season, there was a commotion on the porch. I heard boxes dropping, and then I heard giggling and whispering.

"Shhhh! Straighten up. Dorothy doesn't like drinking."

I peered out the window. There stood Aunt Jean, with another boyfriend, her clothes and hair in disarray. And Aunt Jean and her boyfriend seemed to be propping each other up! I can still see the look of horror on my mom's face when she opened the door.

"Dorothy, I'd like to introduce you to my friend. . . Peaches & Cream," my aunt slurred. She then lost her balance and nearly fell off the porch!

Mom took one look at them and slammed the door.

"Aw, come on, Dorothy. Don't be like that. I have the

childrens' Christmas presents. I'm sorry, really I am." Aunt Jean tried her best to talk straight, through giggles, but I knew that door was not opening. The boxes were left on the porch, and I'm not sure at what point or by whom they were retrieved.

As a young teen, I began to notice my aunt always seemed to be in a better mood than others. I had no way of knowing at the time that the mood came from a bottle. I enjoyed her—most of the time.

At my grandfather's funeral, Aunt Jean arrived at the family gathering, two sheets to the wind, and talking loudly. I watched with fascination as different family members tried to shush her. The living room was wall-to-wall with relatives and friends, so I dared not giggle. I made my way across the crowded room to the bathroom, but before I could close the door, Aunt Jean yelled, "Leave the door open, Bobby, show them what you got!" I froze, hoping they hadn't heard her. My older cousins' roaring laughter removed all hope. I closed the door, thinking I could never come out again! I was too embarrassed.

I forgave her, and as she aged, Aunt Jean mellowed. She continued to look after family members and even turned to gardening in her senior years. Her gardens were a sight to behold, with the local newspapers running stories on her prize-winning yard. But age and alcohol soon took their toll and her gardens and home fell into disrepair.

Aunt Jean also turned into a hoarder. She lived a state away and my visits were infrequent. On one of my last visits to her home, I could see a problem in the making. She showed me her treasures and spoke of so many children without proper clothing or shoes. I began to understand what was driving her compulsion. Her nieces and nephews were all grown, and with senility creeping in, along with hearing loss, she had locked into caretaker mode. She was still collecting clothes for the children—and for me.

As Aunt Jean's memory and living conditions deteriorated, someone did step in to help. I received a call that she was locked up in a psychiatric ward, and I was not surprised. After her evaluation, I spoke with her doctors about her capabilities. They were placing her in a state-funded nursing home in another town. This would be a death sentence to my free-spirited aunt, so I asked for time to find a place for her near me.

Aunt Jean happily agreed, saying she would do anything to get out of there. But as we crossed the Arkansas line, she pleaded to go to my house instead. I explained to her that we only had one bedroom, but as she became more distraught, I agreed.

This began a three-month period of my husband and me sleeping on a sofa bed and sharing our home with Aunt Jean. I came to a full understanding of the Charles Dickens' quote, "It was the best of times; it was the worst of times."

Looking back, I have fond memories of Aunt Jean feasting on scrambled eggs, toast and her favorite jam. She shared stories of early family history—some of it dark—which helped me to understand her need to drink. She would retire to "her" bedroom early, with her jar of Vicks to help her breathe, and a sweet, "Goodnight."

One evening, we had just pulled out the dreaded sofa bed and settled in to watch TV when we heard this *tap-tap* coming from the bedroom. We muted the TV and listened. *Bang! Bang! Bang!* There it was again, only louder.

I rose from bed to check on her, and that's when I heard her coming down the hall, banging on the wall as she walked. "Deaf as a door nail! Deaf as a door nail!" she muttered, as she made her way to the bathroom. She was testing her level of hearing.

We dissolved into laughter. "Shhh, straighten up, she'll hear us!" It brought back memories of a younger aunt, trying to straighten up, so she could deliver my Christmas presents.

We managed to keep Aunt Jean out of any care facilities with the help of another cousin. She lived out her 86 years maintaining her freedom and passed quietly in her sleep. I shared many of her stories at her funeral—I wanted the town to see someone other than the crazy old lady who went through their trash and drank. She once told me, "I'm no saint—I didn't put in for that job. But I love you."

I've always known that . . . always.

Bobby Barbara and Aunt Jean

# Doing It Right

by
Lawrence D. Elliott

I walked nervously through the parking lot. My legs felt as wobbly as freshly cooked pasta and my heart pounded in my chest like a bass drum—it almost drowned out the clacking sound my cleats made on the decaying asphalt. I was about to participate in my first Little League game.

As I approached the baseball diamond, I passed a group of young guys sitting on top of a hideous purple Impala. They passed around a funny-looking cigarette and each one took a puff.

Entering the gate to the baseball field, I straightened up and tried to walk like a veteran instead of the rookie I was. I could see the stands had already begun to fill, not just with parents and family members, but also with area residents from one of the toughest neighborhoods in San Diego. It was not uncommon for clashes to break out between rival gangs nearby when our team practiced, and I recognized some of those same faces among the spectators.

My eyes caught the wall of a nearby building. On it was a fresh piece of obscene commentary about the mother of someone named Joe. I was really glad I wasn't Joe, because my mom was already in the stands waiting to see me play, expecting me to do my best. She would be upset if she saw the graffiti about Joe's mother.

Mom was born in a farmhouse in the small town of Lillie, Louisiana. Her life was not an easy one. She learned early that nothing was going to be handed to her. She worked to instill this knowledge in my siblings and me. We learned very early in life how right she was.

After our father abandoned us, there were times when we didn't have a place to stay or know where our next meal would come from. But we were never allowed to complain. She'd remind us of what we did have and how some people didn't even have that. For her, self-pity was verboten. It was not only a waste of time, but a misuse of energy.

Mom worked long hours and juggled our little budget to make every end meet as she played economic leapfrog to better job opportunities. Sometimes she wouldn't get home until late at night. But she practiced what she preached—she never complained.

And when I wanted to play Little League, Mom scraped together enough money to pay for a baseball glove, cleats and the registration fee. But it came with a caveat.

"If you're going to do this," she warned, "you're going to do it *right*."

"OK," I eagerly answered.

"You mind your coach. You remember how you're supposed to act."

"Yes, I know."

"Just because things get tough that doesn't mean you just up and quit. That's not how life is."

"I know."

"You don't get to give up because things don't go the way you want. That's not how life works."

"I know," I said, hoping the lecture was over. I just wanted to play.

After a few warm-up catches with a fellow teammate, we all went to the dugout as the coach discussed the line-up with the umpire. As the visiting team, our team would bat first. I would be the second batter.

As the leadoff hitter stood at the plate, I waited in the on-deck circle with my bat as I'd seen so many major leaguers do. I could feel my heart pounding even more when my teammate took a swing at the first pitch.

*Crack!* The ball flew to left-center and the fielder barely had to exert himself to make the catch. First out. It was over that fast.

I approached the plate and stood nervously in the batter's box. My heart was beating even more erratically now and my knees wobbled. The pitcher stood on the mound, went into his windup and hurled the ball across the plate.

"Ball one!" exclaimed the burly umpire in a deep baritone. My body seemed to tremble from the power in his voice. Knowing my mom would be watching, I was glad my back was to the stands. I couldn't bear to look at her.

The pitcher started his windup again. I choked up on the bat. The ball sailed toward the plate and I started to swing. But when the ball reached the plate, I found myself unable to follow through with my swing.

"Strike one!" yelled the umpire.

*Shoot! I should have swung at that one!* I yelled in my head.

I could hear the taunts and comments from the crowd.

"He ain't swinging!" one deep voice barked.

"He's chicken!" shouted a female voice.

The catcher threw the ball back to the pitcher. As I prepared for another salvo from the mound, the catcher yelled to the pitcher, "This dude's scared! You can throw anything!"

That comment made me angry! I was determined to swing at the next pitch, no matter what. I just hoped it would be a good one.

Once again, the pitcher went into his windup. This time, there seemed to be cockiness in his body language and he gave me a sneer when he threw the ball. As it approached, I prepared to swing, just as I'd been taught. The ball made strange serpentine movements as it neared. I swung with all of my might. *Crack!*

From the sound, you might have thought I'd made a solid connection. But you would have been wrong. The sound was of the ball connecting with my knuckles! The bat immediately fell from my hands. I tried not to cry, but the pain was so intense I couldn't fight back the tears. The coach dashed from the dugout, and the crowd softly chattered.

"Can you move your fingers?" the coach asked me as he checked my hands.

"Yeah," I answered.

Then a loud voice pierced the silence: "Don't baby him!"

The coach stopped working on my hands. He looked into

the crowd. He wanted to know to whom the voice belonged.

"Don't baby him!" the voice repeated. "Shake it off!"

"Oh, no," I said under my breath.

Slowly, I turned toward the crowd. There, I saw that everyone was looking at this one person. Every mouth was wide-open with astonishment. Embarrassed, I closed my eyes and only one thought came to mind.

*Oh, God, I knew it!*

The voice was that of my mom.

A grown-up Lawrence
with his mother, 2007

# Nonna's Sage Advice

by
Madeline McEwen

I checked the date on the marriage certificate one more time to be sure. My middle-aged brain made a swift calculation—56 years ago. I turned to my husband, Mike, to break the news.

"That means you were born out of wedlock," I said.

"Give it here," he said, taking the flimsy and yellowing document. He peered at the copperplate writing through his smudged reading glasses. "You're wrong. I was born on January 10th. That's nine months later than the date on Mom's marriage certificate."

"Yes, but pregnancy lasts for 40 weeks, not nine calendar months."

"Maybe," Mike said less confidently. "Perhaps I was premature."

I thought of the photograph album excavated from Nonna's old house in England, stuffed with a lifetime's accumulation of junk. The idiom about a tidy desk and a tidy mind nibbled at a corner of my own mind, but I still loved the cute sepia baby photo. On the back was a note about my husband's mammoth 10-pound arrival.

"Anyway," Mike said, "what does it matter if I'm a bastard? That kind of thinking went out with the ark."

"True, but your mom was around in a different era. How would it have affected her?"

His mom—my mother-in-law and our children's Nonna—had always been an unconventional woman. She was a voracious reader, a crossword enthusiast, a deft and accomplished artist and the only female mountain climber in her village in Italy. But that was a long time ago, before dementia robbed her of those pleasures.

Did I mention she was a terrible tease? She'd tell me how easy it was to raise my four children, her darling grandchildren, those obedient angels. They were unlike her own son, who was a child more troublesome than a dozen ragamuffins. That's why she stuck with a singleton.

Now, checking through all her scattered and abandoned papers, I wondered about her idiosyncrasies. Deaf without her hearing aids, blind without her glasses, Nonna never missed a beat when it came to conversations.

I was used to being teased, but not by an octogenarian. Like the time she told Mike to be a more attentive husband or risk my elopement with a lover. She said it to distract me, the shock factor, and stuck her finger in my arrabbiata sauce on the stove.

"Almost as good as mine," she said of the spicy sauce, dodging my wooden spoon. I didn't smack her, though I was tempted.

After widowhood, she moved from England to California to live with us, as did the dementia—the full-time Italian version. I expect it's common enough. A mother comes to live with her son in his house. Therefore, everything within it was fair game because that's motherhood for you: no privacy, no secrets and no lies.

Despite the limitations of age, Nonna always caught the gist of any situation. She slipped right in, reading the body language and empty spaces between. How did she do it? I shall never know.

I marveled at her timing. Like when her legs finally failed her. At last, the upstairs bedrooms became off limits. I saw this as a blessing in disguise. Once again, privacy would be mine. I wouldn't have to worry about her barging into my bathroom or borrowing my hairbrush or any other of the tiny irritations that drove me to distraction. Or so I thought.

Early one morning, Mike and I were enjoying some quiet adult time in bed when I heard Nonna's familiar gait slowly climbing the stairs. One step, and then another. Was this reality or a dream? Why hadn't she called if she needed me? What could she possibly want at this ungodly hour?

Mike paused, too. Together, we listened to her ever-closer presence. Suddenly, the bedroom door swung open and crashed against the wall. I yanked the huge duvet over my head and held my breath. Mike froze in place, although I could hear his heart pounding like a jackrabbit in the jaws of a trap. It seemed cruel to hide, but essential to become invisible.

She didn't turn on the light and didn't come any farther into the room. She muttered in Italian from the doorway. "Dio li fa, poi li accoppia." Dementia sometimes stole her English.

I waited until the door closed and listened to her retreating footsteps. She padded unsteadily all the way downstairs, along the corridor to the single bedroom at the far end of the house. The lock clicked on her white-painted door. I visualized her inside, returning to her project, turning the worn-out collar on her son's shirt and sewing it by hand, every stitch a labor of love.

We emerged from the duvet, hot and breathless like children at a midnight feast.

"What did that mean?" I asked Mike.

"God makes them," Mike translated, "then mates them."

"Really?" I said. I wasn't looking for a literal translation, but insight into her behavior. "I thought we'd fooled her."

"Actually," he said, "You're missing the point."

"What is the point?"

"It's an Italian phrase about couples destined to be together because they're so eccentric."

"Eccentric?" I squeaked. "Me? That's rich, coming from her," I said, annoyed as usual, but then relented. "Do you think she's OK? Perhaps you should check on her."

"Maybe later," he said, snuggling close. "Now, where were we?"

"Honestly," I said, jumping out of bed, grabbing my robe, "Not now." A mother myself, I didn't like to think of her isolated like a lost soul, confused and disorientated. I hoped she hadn't woken the children, too. Although we'd reached the stage of parenthood where sleepless nights were rare, now we contended with an older generation of insomniacs.

The following morning, on the advice of a friend, I began re-introducing Nonna to her life. Often, tangible objects can ignite memories for the elderly and encourage engagement and conversation. I certainly had enough props. Timing was crucial—midmorning was best when Nonna was rested and unflustered.

I hammered on her door and yelled, clutching some papers to my chest. When there was no response, I returned to the kitchen to fetch batteries for her hearing aid.

Five minutes later, I tried again. She sat in her chair in the sun, darning her son's socks with an old-fashioned wooden mushroom which held the heel securely. She wore her sweet, little-old-lady face, but she didn't fool me for a second. I reminded her who I was—the daughter-in-law.

"Did you marry him then?" she asked innocently, confirming the "who-the-hell-are-you?" expression.

With the preliminary introductions over, I started in earnest. She showed no interest in my papers until I handed her a passport.

"Is that yours?" she said, opening it and peering at the picture.

"No, it's yours."

"I was very pretty, wasn't I?"

"You certainly were." I took the passport from her quickly before she read her date of birth and threw a fit.

I opened an old album and placed it on her lap, pointing to different scenes. "Where was that taken?" I could prompt her all day. She had all the time in the world. She fingered the stack of papers, leafing through the documents like an archeologist. Pausing at the marriage certificate, I saw her struggle to recall something.

She began to tell me a tale, an unfamiliar one. She had a stack of standard stories, maybe 20 that she repeated daily. This story wasn't the one about the stained wedding sheets, a story I couldn't allow her to say aloud at the dinner table with her grandchildren present. Nor was it the one about Mussolini during the war in the youth parade because that would upset her. Instead, she told me a new one about leaving Italy as a newlywed and traveling to England, and the rumors that frothed about her, especially when the baby arrived. Apparently, some wicked people speculated about the period of time that elapsed between the wedding day and the birth. Although, she didn't specify who was responsible for all this idle gossip.

"And how did you handle that?" I asked innocently, not meeting her eye.

"Nothing," she said eyebrows high, palms open wide.

"Didn't you want to put them straight?"

"I pretended I didn't understand English," she shrugged.

"Clever."

"Anyway," she said, "what's it got to do with them? Such a tiny thing. Why do they care?"

*Why indeed*, I wondered.

"They think I am a bad woman," she said, "stealing the fine Englishman, tricking him to marry me."

I felt my face coloring. How could anyone think that about this devoted mother?

"They're all dead now anyway," she said. Which, of course, is true, since she was already 89.

"Besides," she said, "We didn't divorce. None of them were married for years like us."

Diamond anniversaries won't feature in our generation. What more proof could anyone want?

"People think what they think, and then they forget," she said. "But the truth stays safe."

*A good one to remember,* I thought.

"Il buon sangue giammai non può mentire," she said, her glance slipping past me to the door. There, her son appeared with a soppy grin, like a shadow of his father.

"Who's got good blood?" Mike said coming over, knowing I needed a translation, hoping his mother would provide one. She did, after taking his hand in hers. She patted and stroked it with tremors and half-spoken whispers before she collected her thoughts from wherever they'd hidden themselves.

"You're a very lucky woman," she said, looking at me, telling me this same thing for the umpteenth time. *Was she teasing?* I couldn't tell.

She turned to her son, "Good blood always shows itself," she said, love and pride in every wrinkle around her smiling eyes.

Nonna in her youth

# Oh, Daddy!

by
Nancy Hershorin

"Mom," Cindy said in an accusatory voice, "you promised when you and Dad were done with the living room, you would do my room next. But you did Laura and Becky's room instead. It's embarrassing to bring friends home when I have such a crappy bedroom. It isn't fair!"

I sighed and gave my 15-year-old daughter a weary look. Everything we did, or didn't do, embarrassed her or upset her or made her angry. I'd actually been avoiding redecorating her bedroom because I didn't want to deal with her annoying habit of finding fault with everything. A friend suggested I let her decorate her own room, so I sounded out Cindy discreetly. She thought black walls would make a statement. I shuddered and dropped my friend's idea.

My husband, Reuben, and I had bought our large ranch-style home at a reasonable price because it needed updating. We'd redecorated the kitchen first. We put in tile floors, refinished the cabinets and covered the walls with wood from an old barn. It was the talk of the neighborhood and we were proud of it.

But Cindy said the barn wood was too old. The rusty nail holes and places where cows or other animals had worn it down smooth were gross to her. She couldn't understand why we didn't put up new paneling.

Next, we did the living room, taking out a sliding door, putting in a stained-glass window, hiding the stereo speakers behind carpet on the walls and hanging the television by a huge anchor chain from the ceiling. Now the neighbors brought over their friends and relatives to see our house. Cindy said she missed the sliding doors and that the stained glass window didn't let in enough light. Plus, the television was too high.

Our two younger daughters shared a bedroom. We painted and wallpapered their room, put in bunk beds and attached to one wall half of a plastic horse painted to look like a carousel animal. The neighbors brought a new group of people over to see the house and a few asked us to help them decorate their homes. Reuben and I were strutting like peacocks.

Cindy, her nose in the air, said the horse looked stupid on the wall and that she couldn't sleep in a room with all that brightly colored wallpaper.

So when Cindy complained about not getting her room updated, all of this flashed through my mind in a second. I knew it would be a nightmare. "Sweetheart, you don't like anything we've done to the house. I don't want to fix up your room then have you complain forever about it. And I won't paint the walls black just to please you."

She glowered at me. "Can't I make any choices at all?"

"Sure you can. I'd be glad to give you the paint samples that I think are nice and let you pick a color for the walls you like from those. You can pick the carpet color, too." So it was settled, and we made plans to give Cindy's room a makeover.

The next few weeks were fraught with pitfalls for unwary parents. Cindy's moods changed with the paint color she was currently favoring. Momentous decisions were being made over paint and carpet colors. Girlfriends were consulted, their opinions of vital importance. When their opinions were ignored by Cindy, feelings were hurt and tears were shed. All my daughter could say was, "Mom, I'm going to have to live with these choices for years and years." I sincerely hoped not.

Finally, the room was finished in yellow and green and outfitted with twin beds. Decorating additions I thought were cute were turned down with a frown. Conformity had to be maintained. The carpet was being installed that day and Cindy was having her friends over to see the room after school. Of course nothing ever goes as planned. The carpet installers removed the bedroom door to install the carpet and didn't put it back because the carpet was too thick. They informed me that the bottom of the door would have to be trimmed down first, and then they left.

I knew Cindy would be upset if she couldn't go in her newly decorated room and shut the door for privacy with her friends. So I called her father at work and asked him to come home early and fix the door.

Reuben had been home just long enough to set up two sawhorses in the hallway and bring in his power saw from the garage. Then Cindy and her friends arrived, bringing along two tall gangly boys with BO and bad complexions. As the four girls came into the house, whispering and giggling, the boys followed behind with apologetic looks. I spared them a moment of pity, remembering my high school days. As I shut the door, I saw my neighbors across the street coming over as well. *Good grief!* I thought. *This is ridiculous.* But being the gracious hostess, I waited and let them in, too.

"Saw the carpet people leave a while ago, Nancy. Thought we'd come over and see what else you've done to the house."

"Nothing much this time, Ed. Just carpet and paint for Cindy's room."

"Well, let's just take a look-see," he said, giving me a hearty slap on the back. I managed a weak smile as they passed me.

There was chaos in the hall with six teenagers, daughters Laura and Becky, Ed and his wife, and our dog Woochie all milling around the doorway to Cindy's room. Standing in the middle by the sawhorses was poor Reuben, clutching his power saw and looking uncomfortable. I think it was the teenage boys that got to him.

He cleared his throat and a look of determination crossed his face. "All right, everyone back away. I want to trim down the door so I can get these sawhorses out of the hall." He radiated confidence and efficiency. Cindy and her friends went into her bedroom—I could see them talking and looking at everything with admiration. Cindy looked positively radiant. I sighed with relief.

When the saw kicked on, Woochie took off like a shot down the hall and sawdust flew as Reuben ran the saw across the edge of the door. In a second, he was done. Putting down the saw, he picked up the door and with Ed's help, he fitted it onto the hinges. He tried to open the door into the bedroom, but it dragged on the carpet so more needed to be taken off. Reuben cut more from the door, and then with everyone watching and Ed helping, the two men put the door back onto the hinges. It was still too low. Reuben scratched his head, looking puzzled and embarrassed.

Suddenly Cindy gave a frantic screech from inside her bedroom. "Daddy, you cut off the top of my door!" We all looked up. It was true.

"Oh, Daddy!" Laura said with a giggle. There was a tense silence as Reuben, who I knew was biting back numerous swear words, turned the door around and put it back in again. It cleared the carpet but the latch wasn't at the same height as the strike plate and the door couldn't close properly. His face went white and his lips formed a frozen smile as he took the door off the hinges and took it out to the garage. None of us said a word.

For once, Cindy had the sense to keep her mouth shut. Ed and his wife left quickly, not saying much and so did Cindy's friends. Reuben stayed out there for a while banging things around, mumbling to himself. Cindy didn't get her door fixed that day.

The door incident became one of those "Remember When" family stories that are told over and over, until so much time had passed that even Reuben could laugh about it.

Cindy, Teen Miss Fresno County (CA), 1975

# Musky-in-Law

by
## Jim Tobalski

I rowed the weathered wooden boat around the quiet cove in front of our Wisconsin cabin. A contrasting mixture of white pine and maple trees cast long shadows on the water's smooth surface as the sun began to hide below the horizon.

Between each rowing motion, I managed to cast my rod and reel, going through the motions the way lazy anglers do as they conclude their fishing day. My mother-in-law sat stoically near the bow, tuckered out from an exhausting day in the sun. Approximately 30 minutes before, I volunteered to take her on an early-evening tour of the bay's shoreline, lined with blooming lily pads, plush vegetation, several blue herons and freshly built beaver huts.

I offered my rowing services to create some quality bonding time with my most important in-law. Between strokes and casts, we exchanged small talk about the Green Bay Packers' offensive line, the chances of an early frost, explanations for my wife's mediocre meatloaf and the value of more grandchildren. Every now and again, I would lob my lure toward shore just to hear the sound of it plopping into the lake's quiet surface. The fish stopped biting my line about three years ago, so I simply enjoyed the rhythmic cadence of each cast and retrieve.

Then *BAM!* I snagged a torpedo.

The unexpected force of the strike jostled my body and jettisoned my favorite Wisconsin Badger baseball cap into the lake. For a split second, I considered throwing my fishing pole overboard because the violent action immediately overpowered me.

Monofilament line screamed from my reel as the underwater missile contorted and bent the tip of my rod beneath the boat. Within seconds, the fish destroyed my confidence and exposed my ineptitude. I was severely overmatched. My fishing equipment could handle a modest-sized largemouth bass, but not the submarine tangled at the end of my line. Then the fish flexed its ego and bolted out of its element, splashing high into the cool evening air. I swore the beast winked at me as he began a headfirst descent back into the lake.

The next 30 minutes raced by as man and mother-in-law battled the sea creature from the pristine lagoon. The fish went by the species' name "muskellunge" or "musky" for short. They combine size, ferociousness and incredible strength. And they've got teeth like a bucksaw. Each year muskies send hundreds of anglers to the emergency room for puncture wounds and lacerations.

Professional anglers travel from all over the world to pursue the great muskies of the Northwoods. Some musky fishing experts don't even experience a nibble during fishing season, but I lucked into hooking one during a social float with my other mom.

The musky on the end of my line measured 45 inches or so from lips to tailfin and weighed between 20 and 30 pounds. If you're impressed, don't be. The Wisconsin record measured 63.5 inches and weighed 69 pounds, 11 ounces, making mine a pup.

During the first half-hour of struggle, my mother-in-law patiently watched me battle the fish. She occasionally marveled at the musky's enormous size. Her comments enhanced the spontaneous daydream being acted out inside my head, which featured me on the front page of the *Wausau Daily Herald* holding Moby Dick. I imagined all of my old high school girlfriends reading the headline at their kitchen tables while sitting across from their husbands who now seemed exceptionally uninteresting and utterly inferior compared to me.

Every so often, my mother-in-law wrinkled her forehead and turned down the corners of her lips when my PG-13 profanity echoed across the cove. But I was entitled to my rants because the fish was pissing me off. I hoisted the lunker near the water's surface then helplessly relented as he dove back to the depths, a sequence the fish and I repeated over and over again. My wrists began to ache, the sky grew darker and karma started to favor the fish. That's about the time my mother-in-law started offering advice, the kind that might normally sound supportive, except during situations involving life and death, such as my epic struggle with the evil musky.

"I don't think you should let him swim under the boat. Your line might snap or get tangled around an oar," she expertly observed.

I bit my bottom lip. The self-induced pain disrupted the neurons that were proceeding to my cerebral cortex, neurons that would have converted thoughts into really stupid, ill-advised words. Instead, all of that cranial activity short-circuited like an electric toaster thrown into an overflowing bathtub. My ears produced visible smoke. Yet my mother-in-law continued.

"Babe Winkelman on Channel 9's Saturday morning fishing show always keeps the tip of his rod pointed toward the front of the boat. Why don't you try that?"

In my mind, I jabbed a fillet knife into my right thigh, deep enough so just the handle showed. The pain prevented me from speaking a toxic rebuttal. Babe Winkelman was a professional fisherman. His popular television program featured Babe himself catching a boatload of fish every week and offering advice on lures, equipment and surefire strategies for catching the big ones. My mother-in-law loved his show. I hated it. Babe was a pompous ass, not because of his arrogance, but because he caught fish—lots of them. And I didn't.

Over the next few minutes, I began to gain ground on the musky. I hoisted and reeled, hoisted and reeled, and the load seemed to lighten. We hadn't seen the beast for about 15 minutes or so. As my mother-in-law and I stared over the side of the boat into the crystal-clear lake, a faint image formed beneath the water's surface, first like a phantom then a blurry semblance and finally like a trophy polished in amazing detail. The musky floated up, suspending itself about a foot below the surface.

"He's huge!" yelled my mother-in-law.

Yes, he was. And handsomely beautiful, with his deep-green coloring and the menacing tiger-like stripes tattooed in his skin from head to tail. He looked tired, so I nonchalantly reached for the net. But with an effortless flick of his tailfin, the king of freshwater fish plummeted back to the depths.

At that very moment, I gave myself a silent pep talk. I

needed a better plan since my current strategy of trying to exhaust him was instead leaving me tired and drained of hope. And now mosquitoes joined us along with lightning bugs and dusk. I would only get one more chance. So I turned and locked eyes with my mother-in-law.

"The next time I hoist him up to the surface, you need to slowly slip the net under his belly and lift with all of your might. I'll quickly lay down my rod and help you heave him into the boat. Can you do that? We've got only one shot at this!"

"Sure I can," she said confidently. "But the net's too small—he won't fit."

"HE'LL FIT!" I lashed back. "I mean, he'll fit," I repeated, softening my tone in hopes that gentler words might bolster confidence and rapport. She was my only hope. If the two of us pulled this off, we'd rewrite history. No mother-in-law and son-in-law have ever successfully landed a trophy fish together, under these circumstances, with so many disadvantages tearing at their fragile states of mind.

The defining moment arrived. I began to methodically crank my fishing line and hoist my rod, each time lifting the musky closer to the surface. He felt petrified. The tip of my fishing pole strained—I expected it to snap like a dry twig. Every now and then I could feel the fish struggle, but with less fury than 30 minutes earlier. Then the visage reappeared beneath the lake's surface, only larger this time. He seemed to be growing exponentially with each passing minute.

I softly but authoritatively commanded my mother-in-law. "Get the net ready now—this is my last chance. When he floats to within about 6 inches of the surface, quickly slide the net under his belly and scoop him into it."

Adrenaline surged throughout my body. Even my teeth pulsed with excitement. I have never been more alert in my entire life. The musky finally came within plain view, looking feeble and defeated by my dominance and skill.

I signaled my assistant. "Now!"

She reacted quickly, but not accurately. She thrust her arms toward the musky, clubbing him over the head with the net's metal frame. The assault transformed him from a lifeless carcass into an atomically charged organism. He leapt straight out of the lake, snapped my line and re-entered with a massive belly flop. The splash reached my eyebrows and chin. My fishing pole felt weightless.

He vanished.

I don't often curse, but this situation seemed like a worthy exception. I managed to avoid the really nasty four-letter profanity, but I invented some new, never-heard-before combinations that made my tirade more profane than each individual word. I directed my outburst at the water, the very spot where the musky last surfaced and made a conscious effort to ignore my mother-in-law.

After exhausting my vocabulary, I sulked and stared into the maturing sunset, hoping God might speak to me and explain the meaning of life. Then a voice broke the silence, but not the Almighty's.

"Babe Winkelman reels the fish all the way to the surface before trying to net it. I think you should have waited another second or two."

For a very brief period—about 15 seconds or so—I imagined tying the anchor around her neck and knocking her overboard. I calmed down, however, and my rage subsided. I now only desired to ignite her hair on fire with outboard motor oil, a plausible accident unlike my initial fantasy.

I decided to return to shore. I rowed calmly, in a manner exactly opposite of how I felt. During the remaining three days of our Northwoods' cabin vacation, my mother-in-law replayed my failure in excruciating detail.

I realize today that my mother-in-law enjoyed telling the story over and over again, because the moment demanded immortalization. And I'm not mad anymore. But I occasionally catch myself daydreaming about Babe Winkelman, wishing him months of public humiliation after being arrested while fishing with an expired license.

In retrospect, my mother-in-law was right. I should have watched more of Babe's television shows. Damn, he was good!

Jim . . . but that's not his mother-in-law!

# Mother Knows Best

My mama told me . . .

# The Real Facts of Life

by
Laura Edwards-Ray

Madison is high strung, anxious, naïve, goofy and pretty damn cute.

The public school she and her sister attend has a life skills class in the fourth and fifth grades that explains the basic facts of life. I had been asking my 11-year-old Madison every day after school if she wanted to talk about anything—if she had any questions about anything—hoping and praying she would say, "No." I thought she was just too embarrassed to ask, and being the weasel mother that I am, I responded with a silent, *Thank you, God!* when she said she had no questions.

A few months later on a gorgeous Saturday afternoon, both girls were content sitting in the back seat of our car, listening to Raffi on the CD player as we were driving home from somewhere. It could have been swim class, Hebrew school, Girl Scouts, soccer, pottery class, Shakespeare for Children, underwater basket weaving . . . they all seem to endlessly run into each other. That's when, right out of the blue, Madison said, "Mom?"

"Yes, Madison. What is it?"

She said with a huge sigh, "Well, I just want you to know that I know that it's not just God who is making those babies!" She then gave me this goofy little finger-snap-point-wink.

My younger daughter Morgan looked at her strangely, like always, and said, "Mommy, what *is* she talking about?"

I quickly replied, "I don't know, honey. But when we get home, why don't you go over to the Wilsons' house to play with Michael and David. And Maggie, we'll go into the bed-room and you and I can talk." At the same time, I was think-ing, *Oh no, I guess it's time for THAT talk!*

When we got home, Morgan skipped down the street, oblivious to the fact that I was ready to finally have "the talk" with her older sister. Fearing a nervous breakdown, I thought how great it would be to just insert an I.V. of tequila into my arm right at that moment.

Madison walked into the room, with a Cheshire-Cat smirk.

I said, "OK, honey, why don't you sit on the bed and tell me what exactly you were talking about in the car?"

She looked at me with such excitement in her eyes, as if she knew something that the whole, entire world was just waiting to hear. She said, "Oh, Mom, I know now!"

"OK, tell your mommy what you know."

"Well, I know that the mommy has the egg and the daddy has the sperm and when they kiss, they can make a baby!" She was so thrilled by this exciting newsflash—I was waiting for her to shout, "Quick! Let's call CNN and talk to Wolf Blitzer right away!"

I didn't want to break her heart, and I did absolutely love the fact that she prefaced her discovery with the words "mommy" and "daddy." I wanted to give her that little snap and wink thing right back for that one. But instead, I looked at her and in my kindest, most loving way possible, I said, "Oh, Madison, you can't get pregnant by kissing a boy."

She looked at me puzzled, thought a while and replied, "Well, then, where does the man's sperm come from?"

"Honey, the sperm comes from a man's penis."

She then looked at me, and turned as pale as I've ever seen her—and she is a pale kid to begin with.

"OH, MOMMY. PLEASE, PLEASE DON'T TELL ME . . ."

I was a little frantic at this point, and I screeched, "Tell you what, honey?"

She screamed, "OH, MOMMY, PLEASE DON'T TELL ME THAT I'M GOING TO HAVE TO KISS A PENIS!"

I have a feeling that I may have screamed so loud at this point during our very mature conversation that people in Peoria could have heard me. "NOOooo, ABSOLUTELY NOT!"

And then, I added very softly under my breath, "Only, of course, if you want jewelry."

# Standing My Ground

by
## Lisa McManus Lange

Envision, if you will, a red-haired maiden, with her hair blowing in the wind and her corsets drawn tight to enhance a youthful bosom. She stands firm with her sword raised above her head, ready for battle. With her stern gaze on her opponent, fending off the demon before her is the only thing on her mind.

In a swirl of cloud and pixie dust, technological enemies dance and taunt the sword-wielding maiden—iPods, Xboxes, computers, cellphones, DVDs, Game Boys—intertwining like venomous snakes. Standing behind her are two boys with their arms outstretched, asking the enemies to help them, to save them.

It's just another day at the Lange household, another day of Mom versus technology.

Not only am I the minority in the house of three men— two sons and a husband—but I am also the minority in the quest to limit the amount of time all three of their faces are hypnotized by various screen sizes.

I like to consider myself technology-adequate in today's world. For example, when my oldest son received an iPod for Christmas, so did I. And while I know I am contradicting myself, I'll be honest—I LOVE IT! To fend off writer's butt, I take many walks and my iPod is connected to my head—masterfully picked songs urge my steps harder, faster. And our dual iPods lend to mother/son bonding as we compare songs, swapping and exchanging tunes.

Back in my day, Atari and ColecoVision were huge. I was an expert at a game called *Xaxxon* and was always sporting a "Coleco-finger." There was *Pac-Man*, a cartoon character we could control at a whim, and when I was 16, I finally received my own phone and a Walkman. As I write this, I'm on a laptop. This makes me wonder if I was as technologically driven as my kids when I was a kid. Or worse yet, am I just like my tech-crazy family? I resolve that I am not like them; I am not addicted to technology.

All contradictions aside, I soldier on. I am trying to protect my lovely family's minds from turning to mush. As the daily battle continues, three male voices echo each other when I call them to come to the dinner table in the evenings. I usually get a flurry of responses, the most common being, "I'll be right there! I'm about win. Just wait!"

My fantasy rebuttal? *I don't care if you're online with people from Mars! Dinner is ready, and I mean NOW!* But I don't say that because part of my quest is to exemplify calm, rational, *mature* behavior.

As any parent would do, I worry about schoolwork, social

interaction and couch-potato butt. I have enough of that for everyone. There are days when I threaten that if they don't get off that so-and-so technological gadget, I will throw it onto the nearby highway. They immediately get the hint and listen.

Wow! They do listen . . . sometimes.

One son is a preteen and the other is in his teens. The upcoming years are going to challenge me beyond any game of Pac-Man, and I must up the ante. I require them to read books until they are cross-eyed. And even worse, I ban electronic games for the entire day. Then I kick them outside to do something—anything. After disgruntled mumbles by the two, they relent. And, lo and behold, they usually enjoy being outside.

As you can figure out by now, I am the protector of my family. I am diligent. I never give up and never back down. Picking your battles works, and when it comes to technology, I set time limits and stick to them.

One spring break when I was already dreading the technological war sure to erupt with all that time off from school, I set one of those time limits. Needing to run some errands, I gave my three "e-boys"—as I call them—a warning: "When I get back, everything goes off. Understood?" All three hypnotized faces barely registered that I was leaving the house. Their Xbox game on the big screen was too captivating.

We live less than a block away from a nature sanctuary that has trails, bridges and a pond, home to countless ducks. A world in its own, the natural escape provided countless memories of year-round walks and duck-feeding expeditions when my two sons were younger. But since age and technology has taken over my boys' bodies and minds, coaxing them to go feed the ducks had become more and more challenging.

On the way to run errands, I passed the sanctuary. There I was forced to stop for some ducks who decided to cross the street. As I impatiently waited for them to waddle by, they gave me an idea—bless their little hearts. I was going to drag my little gamers by their earlobes to the park.

Skipping my errands, I turned around and raced home. Once inside the house, orders were issued: "Coats on! Shoes on! Hit the bathroom, if you need to. Let's GO!" My promises of visiting the park for only a few minutes were barely audible through their complaining. I had to literally drag all three of them to the sanctuary, and I swear, pieces of running shoes trailed behind us as my boys dragged their toes. Even my husband was upset and didn't want to go. The way they carried on, you'd think I was forcing them to clean the toilets with their toothbrushes.

But inch by inch, foot by foot, their steps lightened and in no time, they were walking normally. *Are they remembering our countless trips to our little oasis, back in the olden days when they were just kids?* I thought to myself. As we neared our destination, their cheeks brightened with color and their eyes lit up at the realization that there is a world outside our four walls!

As the ducks raced to us—the crinkling of our bags of bread urging their waddles—I watched in fascination as my sons regressed into the easily entertained children they once were. And even my husband was having a great time. When I announced later it was time to head home, there were protests to stay a bit longer.

Things will change eventually, I know. But for now, all I can do is stand my ground and enjoy the moments. And never relinquish my sword.

# The Power of Suggestion

by
Sylvia Bright-Green

When I hung up the telephone, I thought to myself, *If it rings once more with another bickering family member, I'll send out an SOS to extraterrestrials to beam their 'seedlings' aboard!*

Don't get me wrong—I love my family. But their litany of complaints has had me feeling that maybe my having a nervous breakdown is the only means of relaxation. Grandmother always said, "Why rush to marry and have kids? Because with little tads come petty bads, but with big toads come heavy loads."

I should have listened to her words of wisdom. My four children have been arguing with each other ever since they learned to grunt. And now that they're older, they have word duels with each other:

"Bro, I'm trying really hard to imagine you with a brain."

"Gawd! Sis, you look like a graveyard. Is that the style now?"

"Well, bro—at least I'm smart enough to know which

end to wear my pants on."

Whenever they attempt to drag me into their feuds, I remark, "Back off. You're standing in my aura where I'm trying to live happily ever after." But they never get the message. They just continue to complain.

I truly believe that when you have older children, it's best they live out of state. Then, when they phone crying or yelling or begging for anything, you can say, "ETs (Eccentric Transplants) don't phone this home. Your home isn't planetary."

Suddenly, the ringing of the phone interrupted my thoughts.

"Geez!" I blurted out. "I'm not even over yesterday, and here they're dragging me into today." Immediately, rage began to hotly pulse through my veins, transforming me into a hulking monster. I felt my blouse expand, popping all six buttons one by one. Then my pantyhose split, sending a runner to my toes.

"Gosh darn!" I shouted. "Now look what happened to my last pair of pantyhose. Why don't I just disconnect this blasted telephone?" But knowing my family, they would hop into their cars and drive to my back door.

Picking up the phone, I bellowed, "Your mother isn't here! She's been abducted by ETs who want to make sure she can't reproduce anymore!"

After a slight pause, I hear, "Hello, is Karen Ann Green there?"

"Who is this?" I rudely replied.

"Madam," the man quickly responded, thinking that I might hang up on him, "I'm the Army recruiting officer in your area. I thought that since Ms. Karen is 18 and a graduate, perhaps she would be interested in a career in the United States Army."

*Hmmm. That sounds good to me,* I thought. So I listened to the masculine voice talk about the benefits Karen could receive if she enlisted.

During his speech, wild thoughts bounced around in my mind. *Wouldn't it be nice if I could get all my fighting family into different branches of the Armed Services? Then all of our big country clashes could become small backyard bashes.*

"Sir," I said, breaking into his oration. "Would a 22-year-old daughter who's great at KP—and I mean kitchen police, but Kung-fu punching—be eligible?"

"Yes," the officer hesitantly replied.

"Say, could you also use a strong 18-year-old who's first-rate at digging trenches with one rip on his Honda? What about a pedal-to-the-metal, hot-rod sister who can clear a wooded terrain with her little Toyota?"

Before the officer had a chance to respond, I picked up mental speed and slipped him another idea. "What about a 60-year-old mother-in-law who'd make an excellent drill sergeant?"

*Great! I'm almost home free . . . just a few more agitators to go.*

"Sir, is it possible, for sanity's sake, that you could be persuaded to take a listless husband who you trained during the Korean War to sleep at the drop of his helmet? And a hyperactive 14-year-old who knows Army expletives? Or a psychotic poodle whose aim is good?"

When I finished, I heard a familiar sound coming from the phone. It was the same auditory sensation I now give my feuding children—dead airtime.

# Leaving My Mark

by
Sioux Roslawski

When I noticed a Spitfire skateboarding logo tattooed onto my 18-year-old son's belly, I became a raging spitfire. The tattooed face featured a devilish grin, a winking eye and leaping flames for hair. I wasn't happy, but I kept it under control.

Months later, I saw my son had a new penguin tattoo on his shoulder blade. *Ugh!* I thought.

Ian's next tattoo was a surprise: he had two Chinese characters emblazoned across his upper chest. According to him, the symbols stood for "integrity" and something else—I can't recall what. Since Ian couldn't read Chinese, for all he knew the characters could have read, "idiot" and "lazy slug." And yet, our son remained proud of his new embellishments.

Ian's next tattoo was the phrase "Dying 2 Live" inked on his forearm. *Live?! If this kid keeps on, he's going to die because I'm ready to kill him!* Yes, I was becoming more and more frustrated.

Ian's father and I begged our son to hold off on getting any more tattoos. But he didn't listen. When Ian returned home from college during the holidays, he not only showed off his dean's list grades, but another new "tat," as well.

So one year, when Ian was home for a quick visit, I offered him the best holiday gift request ever: "Ian, you know what I want for Christmas? No more tattoos. How cheap a gift that is, right?" My eyebrows rose hopefully and my eyes bugged out as I tried to shoot my message his way. Unfortunately, he ignored my suggestion and came home for the holidays with a new tattoo.

Desperate, my husband and I tried backing our concerns about his excessive tattoos with scientific proof: "Ian, no more tattoos, please, until the frontal lobe of your brain finishes developing. That'll happen when you're 23 or 24. Then, if you still want another tattoo, you'll be mature enough to make an informed decision." He thought we were joking. But his father and I were not laughing.

For the next few years, all three of us waved the white flag of surrender. We didn't harp about new "skin art" and Ian got no new body embellishments. I was proud of my son, because getting a new one would have been so easy for him. All he'd have to do was call his brother-in-law Jason. Our daughter is married to an award-winning tattoo artist and painter. Jason would have inked Ian at the family discount rate. But Ian never asked him. My hopes soared—maybe our son actually listened to us?

Ian graduated from college with honors. Soon after, he came home and sat his father and me down for a serious chat.

Ian told us he was well aware of the sacrifices we had made over the last four years, from little gestures like slipping money into his checking account when it dipped too low, to the ultimate biggie—taking out a loan to pay his tuition.

In a very grateful tone, Ian said to us, "Mom, Dad, I want to permanently honor you." Then he raised his shirt and pointed. "Right here. I'm going to have a portrait of you guys tattooed onto my chest."

Using the best arsenal we could muster, the two of us shot back with pleas on why his offer wasn't a good idea. Determined to go through with his tattooed tribute to us, Ian refused to listen, that is until I came up with the ultimate blow: "Ian, no girl is going to want to have sex with you if your parents are staring at her the whole time."

For once, our son—the college graduate—listened to us.

Ian and a few of his tats

# When Hummingbirds Call

by
Bud Gardner

"You need a hummingbird feeder, Buddy," my mom said. "If you hang a hummingbird feeder, they will come."

"Mom, it won't work. I've hung four feeders at different times over the years, and not a single hummingbird has ever come to visit. I don't think they like me."

She gave me a stern look, the one I'd seen all my life. Goldie Gertrude Trimmer Gardner was a tough, stoic woman who had spent 40 years teaching in one-room schoolhouses on the high plains of western Kansas.

"Well, I'm going to buy you one anyway." End of discussion. And off she went.

Mom and my dad, Pat Gardner, were on a two-week summer visit. The first time they'd made the long drive from the Midwest to California was during the 10-year period I'd taught physical education and coached at a college in the Sacramento area. During this trip—the second to California to visit me and my family—I was the assistant dean of students at another college in south Sacramento.

A couple of hours later, Mom was back.

"There, now they'll come," she said triumphantly. "Buddy, you must keep the feeder full of red liquid food because hummingbirds will drink half their body weight in sugar each day. Did you know that?"

"Mom," I snapped. "Sure I knew that. Don't you remember, I taught biology for three years?"

"Humph! Maybe you should have paid more attention in your ornithology class."

Before I could respond, she waved me off, beaming. Just then, out of the blue, a hummingbird appeared and drank deeply from the red juice in Mom's new feeder. Then a second, third and fourth showed up, fluttering and drinking.

"Did you see that, Buddy? The one hummingbird ran off a couple others. He must be the dominant one. They're very territorial, you know."

"I knew that, Mom."

"You keep the feeder full, and you'll have hummingbirds like flies."

Over the next few days, the hummingbirds established a base in our large bush in the corner of the backyard and made a beeline to and from the bush to the feeder. I couldn't believe it. I couldn't keep the feeder full. They drank the red liquid faster than I could fill it.

Mom's parting shot as they drove away heading back to Kansas was, "Remember, keep that feeder full."

"OK, Mom. You win."

I was shocked when I returned to the patio. The hummingbirds were gone. The feeder remained full for days, but not one single hummingbird showed up ever again. I gave up and chalked it up to a surreal experience. Besides, I had to go back to work.

A week later, I was back on the job. It was the first week of fall semester, and I was on my knees in a storage room, painting a welcome sign for incoming freshmen. When I stood up to admire my work, I accidentally bumped a 4-foot-tall standing roll of butcher paper. It slammed into a huge coffee pot and dumped gallons of scalding coffee on my lower right leg. The excruciating pain was so intense I couldn't talk.

In a panic, I pulled up my pants leg and ripped off a slab of burned flesh the size of my hand. Shuddering, I staggered into the office and somehow blurted out, "Help!" My secretary quickly called 911. It took a trip to the hospital and shot of morphine to calm me down.

"You've got a third-degree burn there, Mr. Gardner," said the emergency room doctor. "Stay off that leg for at least a month. You're going to have a lot of pain for a few weeks."

Back home, I struggled. I fought the pain and put undue stress on my wife. She was under the gun. Over the course of those first two weeks, she cooked, bandaged my wound, took care of our two daughters and taught elementary school. To say she was stressed out is an understatement. Then the unexpected happened.

One evening, my wife answered the front door and she burst into tears. There stood duty-bound Goldie and Pat. Mom took over. She cooked meals, got the girls off to school, helped them with their homework and changed the bandages on my leg. A week later, I was able to sit up. The pain greatly lessened.

A few days later, we were enjoying the sun on the patio when my mom scolded me.

"Look, Buddy, you let the hummingbird feeder get empty. No wonder you haven't had any hummingbirds here."

"Mom, believe me, that was the last thing on my mind."

"I'll fill the feeder so we can get them back."

"Fat chance," I grumbled.

She'd no sooner filled and hung the feeder when one, two, three and what seemed like dozens of hummingbirds flooded the feeder once again.

"See, I told you so. You've got to keep that feeder full, and they'll come."

I watched in amazement.

A week later, my folks returned to Kansas. When they left, the hummingbirds left, too, never to return.

Across the years, I have hung three different types of feeders and filled them with a variety of commercial and home-made red sugar-based liquids, but not a single hummingbird has ever taken a drink. Mom had this divine ability to attract them to her. I know, because when I placed a bouquet of sun-flowers at my parents' gravesite this summer, within seconds a hummingbird hovered, checked out the sunflowers, and then flew away.

Oh, by the way, I am never without hummingbirds now. As a tribute to Mom, I bought an expensive, elegant, metal front door screen which displays one dynamic hummingbird in full flight, drinking from a flower.

And Mom, I never have to worry about feeding hummingbirds ever again.

Bud and his metal hummingbird he never has to feed

# Killing Them with Kindness

by
Terri Elders

The doorbell clanged. "Gonna answer that?" Mama asked, frowning at me from the kitchen as I scuttled down the hall toward the back bedroom I shared with Sissy.

"It's Cathy and Sheila from school. I'm scared. I'm going to go read about the Wars of the Roses."

The doorbell shrilled again, followed by a thunderous *rat-a-tat-tat*. Mama shook her head and sneaked a quick peek at the cake baking in the oven. She whipped off her apron, fluffed up her hair and strode toward the door.

"Roses can wait," she said. "Just sit down on the sofa and don't say a word!"

"Be careful," I called after her, "Everybody calls them 'Spit Cat' and 'She Wolf.' They're bad news."

"Good afternoon, ladies," Mama trilled, welcoming the menacing duo on the doorstep as if they'd been expected tea-time guests. "How are you today?"

Cathy stepped forward, hands clenched at her sides, eyes squeezed to slits. I half expected her to hiss and raise a claw. "We've got a beef with your daughter," she said.

"What did Terri do?" Mama cast a puzzled glance at me. I hardly posed a threat to anybody. Because I'd skipped a grade, my sister and I had just started junior high together. But unlike fully developed Sissy, I still sucked my thumb behind my textbooks, unless I was busy gnawing my pencils to shreds.

"Not 'Termite,'" Sheila growled, glaring in my direction. "Sissy. She's trying to steal my boyfriend."

I squirmed on the velveteen sofa cushion. If the two did bump off Sissy—who wasn't home at that moment—a jury probably would find it justifiable homicide. Sissy had turned heads since she was six. By the time she hit adolescence, grown men stopped dead in their tracks on the street to stare at her. She'd bat her turquoise eyes, toss her thick head of hazelnut curls and smile back at them like a queen awarding a favor to devoted courtiers.

On the other hand, Sissy might emerge victorious in a down and dirty tiff with these two girls. From our sisterly tussles, I knew the strength in those deceptively slender fingers, well exercised by years of spanning octaves and trilling arpeggios at her upright piano. "Just remember, I'll always be bigger, stronger and prettier," she'd crow, pinning me to the floor.

"She'll be home soon," Mama said, waving the pair in. "You might as well wait inside."

They trudged in without as much as a token swipe of their feet on the welcome mat. Cathy swiveled her head around to take in our post-WWII décor: knickknack shelves stuffed with ceramic elves, embroidered antimacassars lying on the back of the armchairs, a braided rag-rug and Sissy's Spinet piano tucked into the corner. Daddy used to say we barely had room to swing a cat in our minuscule living room. I suddenly pictured Sissy swinging Cathy into one of the whatnots, elves hurtling to the floor. I'd likely be the one scooping up shards and comforting Mama.

Sheila sniffed suspiciously. "What's that I smell?"

I, too, had noticed the rich brown sugary aroma drifting in from the kitchen. I'd nearly forgotten about the cake. Daddy raved about this exceptionally moist, buttery, gooey dessert, and even I, who generally lacked a sweet tooth, appreciated its citrusy tang and caramel crunch.

"Why, ladies, it's pineapple upside-down cake. I was just about to offer you each a piece," Mama said, waltzing back to the kitchen. I knew she had baked that cake for Daddy's Friday supper surprise. But now she returned, clutching a pair of her best Woolworth's pink glass plates, each laden with warm slabs of the treat. Our guests eyed the steamy squares with their pineapple circles and maraschino cherries and licked their lips. Mama and I watched silently as they shoveled full forks into their mouths.

As they forked up the last few bites, Sissy breezed into the house. I stiffened, wondering if I should snatch Mama's beloved plates away from the so-called ladies before Spit Cat and She Wolf hurled them at my sister.

Sissy cast an eyeball at the living room tableaux and didn't wince. "What's cooking?"

Sheila jumped to her feet, clutching her pink plate in both

hands. Mama stepped forward and took it from her. Cathy rose more slowly, stabbing her last cherry and moving it to her mouth. Mama snatched that plate, as well. I exhaled.

"You've been making eyes at Roger and I want it to stop!" Sheila snarled. I well understood how she'd earned the moniker "She Wolf." Her eyes even glittered like a rabid canine's as she tried to stare down my sister.

"Roger?" Sissy said, shaking her head, curls afloat. "Roger's OK in my book, but I'm interested in someone else."

"You were hanging with him this morning by the cafeteria," Sheila continued, not giving in.

"Sure. He was asking me if I could go to a party tomorrow night."

"See?" Sheila howled, turning to Cathy, who in turn glowered at Sissy and raised a balled fist.

"Hey, wait, not as his date, just to play the piano at the Town Club party. It was supposed to be a surprise for you."

Sissy scurried to her piano. "This is the song he wanted," she said, hitting the opening notes to that latest Andrews Sisters hit, *I Can Dream, Can't I?* "He said it was the song that the two of you first danced to this summer, when he realized how crazy he was about you."

Mama's guests exchanged sheepish glances as Sissy sang the haunting lyrics. When she finished, the room remained silent for a few seconds. Then Sissy jumped up, helped herself to a piece of cake and offered more to the visitors.

After wolfing down seconds, Cathy and Sheila thanked Mama profusely for her hospitality and left. Mama and I sighed concurrently.

Sissy hurried to the phone. "I'm lucky there's nobody on the party line," she said, as she dialed.

"Roger? Sheila was here. She saw us together this morning. I said you wanted me to come to the party tomorrow night to play her favorite song at the party. Yes, I think I convinced her. She and Cathy left, all smiles."

When she tucked the receiver back into its cradle, Mama demanded an explanation.

"I can't help it if guys always try to hit on me," Sissy wailed. "It's not as if I invite all that attention." Then she blinked her mascara-laden lids at us and huffed off to our shared bedroom.

*Dang nabbit*, I thought as I washed the dinner dishes that night. Only one little square of pineapple upside-down cake had remained in the pan, and of course it had to be for Daddy. My gorgeous sneaky sister had bamboozled me out of the only dessert I loved.

As always, I forgave her. Whatever trickery Sissy got into, it somehow always seemed worth it if I could hear her sing. Besides, it would be useless to nurse a grudge. She'd always be bigger, stronger and prettier. I could be smarter and sweeter.

Picking up my book on medieval England to read about the Wars of the Roses, I realized that neither Sissy nor I would ever match Mama's beautiful and legendary kindness. Mama would have offered those warring 15th century English Lancasters and Yorks some freshly baked cake or pie. And it might have worked.

# Mom's Best Advice

by
## Sheree K. Nielsen

When I was a child, Mom had a lot to say about a lot of subjects. But three are the most memorable to me:

1. Don't stick foreign objects in your nose or your mouth.
2. Clean your plate because there are children starving in the world.
3. Don't talk to strangers.

Little did I know that her pearls of wisdom would come in handy throughout my lifetime.

### Number 1

Mom often lectured about not sticking things in my nose. "Your cousin shoved a button up her nose, and it got stuck sideways. Aunt Georgia had to rush her to the hospital to have the button removed."

Curious to see if I could obtain the same results as my cousin, I shoved several sunflower seeds into my left nostril. I was four years old at the time and didn't tell anyone.

I had trouble breathing over the next few days. Mom diagnosed me with a sinus infection—or possible blockage—and marched me to the pediatrician's office. With a spelunker's flashlight strapped to his forehead, Doc leaned in for a closer look, nose probe in hand. "Something's up there. Not quite sure what it is. Need to get an X-ray."

The X-ray revealed several tiny almond-shaped objects lodged in my nostril. Doc extracted the suspicious material with a pair of medical tweezers. I felt instant relief.

"Looks like sunflower seeds to me, Mom," said Doc.

Mom's silky beige complexion turned tomato-red. I could tell she was infuriated. My butt would take on the same color of Mom's face after a good old-fashioned spanking due me shortly after we got home. But all she could say at that moment was, "Did you know you could have sprouted?" I heeded Mom's advice and never ever again put foreign objects into my nose.

A few years older and wiser, I loved being outside after a fresh spring rain. After my usual breakfast of cornflakes, I headed to the backyard for my morning ritual of scaling the neighbor's fence. Seven children, barely a year apart, lived next door.

Before setting one foot on the chain link fence, I noticed one of the neighbor kids—three-year-old Connie—sitting spread-eagle under their porch in the mud. She wore a pink frilly dress, and her face was a mud-caked mess. Her chubby fingers excavated in the coffee-colored muck, searching. A worm-like fuzzy insect emerged, a 3-inch-long caterpillar, which she shoved into her pie hole. Half in and half out, the insect dangled from the corners of her mouth.

With every breath in my lungs, I demanded, "Connie, get that bug out of your mouth!"

She stared at me, dumbfounded. After a push with those pudgy fingers and a quick swallow, the bug was gone. To this day, the image of that disgusting caterpillar dangling between Connie's fat baby lips is branded forever in my mind. That's why I NEVER EVER put foreign objects in my mouth.

## Number 2

Mom, a fan of the Clean Plate Club, shared a second with me: "Eat your peas. There are kids starving in the world."

I *hated* peas. At the dinner table, I'd lodge those nasty things inside my cheeks just like a squirrel. When Mom and Dad weren't looking, I'd spit them into my napkin and hide the napkin under my plate. I was brilliant. Sometimes, I'd excuse myself to the restroom, spit the peas into the toilet and flush the green troublemakers away.

Things were brighter when Grandma came to visit. She shared a different philosophy about food: "If you eat everything off your plate, it looks like you're starving," she advised. "Leave a little food. This lets the cook know you enjoyed the meal." I loved Grandma for that. When she joined us for dinner, I'd honor her advice and leave all my peas on the plate.

As a teenager, I became less finicky when trying new vegetables. Spinach, broccoli and Brussels sprouts were my friends. I became a member of the Clean Plate Club when it came to green leafy vegetables. The starving kids could have my peas.

**Number 3**

Mom's last bit of advice is what I remember best: "Don't talk to strangers."

I recall walking home one sunny afternoon from Resurrection of Our Lord Catholic grade school with my friend, Susie. Both nine-year-olds, we looked cute in our Peter-Pan collared shirts, green plaid jumpers, lacy ankle socks and penny loafers as we strolled and skipped down the city streets. Matter of fact, we were so cute that a man in a big white Buick even noticed us. Bare chested, he wore a brown fedora hat.

Slowing to almost a complete stop, he asked, "Do you girls need a ride? I've got candy."

Susie quickly hollered, "Get lost or we'll call the police!" I was impressed with her street smarts. He grinned from ear to ear as he gripped the steering wheel with his left hand. Before he drove off, his right arm made a rapid up and down movement. Puzzled, Susie and I looked at each other then hightailed it home.

Bursting through the front door, I told my parents about our experience with the man in the Buick. After a lecture from Mom and Dad about talking to strangers, I asked, "What was he doing with his right arm?"

"Polishing his stick shift," Dad said.

Well into my 30s, Mom's words of wisdom came in handy. Headed for a doctor appointment at a medical building, I parked my car in a large, ground-level garage. The garage was eerily dark.

Hearing the gritty step of shoes hitting pavement directly behind me, I spun around quickly. There stood a man in a trench coat.

"Hi there. Whatchya doing?" the dark-haired man asked and winked at me.

"Well, I have herpes, and I'm going to see if my doc can give me something for these painful lesions."

Of course it wasn't true, but that statement was enough to freak out the dude. He turned around and walked in the opposite direction. Come to think of it now, maybe he was flirting with me and I missed out on the date of a lifetime.

On many occasions, I'm the one to approach strangers. That's one advantage to being an extrovert. For instance, on a recent visit to Keeneland's annual horse sale in Kentucky, I met the jockey that rode Triple Crown winner Seattle Slew. At an organic farm in Missouri, I chatted with folks from all walks of life at a Sunday supper. One summer, I viewed the transit of Venus through a telescope with an observatory group. I've met local legend and hippie Surfer Pete in the Bahamas, on the island of Eleuthera. I've even struck up conversations with people while strolling along beaches in South Carolina and Georgia and the lakeshores in Wisconsin.

Although Mom is only here in spirit, I'll never forget her

winning smile, positive attitude and pearls of wisdom. Her best advice shaped the person I am today. And, rest assured, Mom, I no longer stick foreign objects up my nose.

Sheree and Mom

# One in a Million

by
## Susan Guerrero

Some women love housecleaning while others would prefer to bake batches of cookies that fill the house with luscious aromas. Then there are those women whose fingers click knitting needles as fast as they can blink their eyes and turn out incredibly soft and beautiful afghans and baby sweater sets with matching booties and hats.

Of course, there are the culinary masters in the kitchen whose meals make people weep with happiness. Their biscuits are flaky. Their turkeys are tantalizing and their mashed potatoes are creamy and topped with little pools of melted butter.

The table settings of the good cooks are usually gorgeous, too, with matching china, sparkling glasses and gleaming silverware. And they never forget the centerpieces.

I have aunts and cousins who can sew entire wardrobes, some without even using patterns. When they see a lovely outfit for themselves or their children in a store, they whisper, "I can make that." And then they do!

How about the women in my family whose talents shine in gardening? They love the feel of dirt under their fingernails. You will often find them on their grimy knees, bent over their beds of cosmos or picking deadheads off their petunias.

My mom—who I called "Mummy"—was like none of these women. She enjoyed reading and music, but they were not her obsessions in life.

Her passion was painting, and I don't mean on canvas. She loved to paint walls and woodwork, staircases and railings and everything in between.

The store in the small town where I grew up had a paint department. Mummy and the manager were on a first-name basis. He knew about her kids and she learned about his wife and family. After all, she was probably his very best customer.

She was there in the heat of summer or the brutal cold of winter. Neither droughts nor hurricanes would deter her from going to that paint department if she were planning a painting project.

The old house my parents bought needed lots of interior painting. However, once a room was painted, that didn't signal that Mummy was finished with it. She changed color schemes like the wind. If the pink bedroom no longer suited her, she'd repaint it baby blue in a few days. If she disliked the way the kitchen came out in yellow, she'd beat a path right back to the paint department and pick out another color. I can still close my eyes and visualize Mummy on a ladder painting a ceiling or the walls of yet another room. There is no possible way to know how many coats of paint the walls of that old house have on them but I'd be willing to bet one would turn up several layers.

While the memory and smell of Mummy's painting ventures are still fresh in my mind, there's one event that stands out more than any other, one that stays with me to this day.

The elementary school we attended was several blocks from our house. After school one day, I trekked home, opened the front door and ran upstairs to the one bathroom in the house. With five girls, it got plenty of use after school.

Just as I sat down to take care of my business, I heard Mummy scream from downstairs, "Don't sit on the toilet!"

I tried to get up, but it was too late. My butt was secured to the freshly painted bright-green toilet seat.

I screamed that it was too late. Mummy was very unhappy I had ruined her paint job, but she wasn't as upset as me. Hanging on to the edge of the bathtub with one hand and the edge of the sink with the other, I hoisted my body up. It was not a pretty sight. Mummy brought me a rag and turpentine so I could remove the evidence.

My sisters heard what had happened and were cackling outside the door like a bunch of Halloween witches. They sang the advertising jingle for a particular brand of canned vegetables. I heard the words, "Jolly Green Giant" bandied about. They sang, "Ho-ho-ho" all evening.

Now whenever I set foot inside a green bathroom, I remember back on that fateful day, a day that has become a family legend. While Mummy's passion for painting was different from most women's, that was OK with me. But now before I sit down, I check the toilet seat.

# CHAPTER SEVEN

# You Just Never Know

Sometimes the unexpected happens,
and it turns out right.

# The Big Announcement

by

## Pat Wahler

Normally I love an invitation to go out. But when our son Justin and his girlfriend Kathy called to ask us to their house for dinner, I had to decline. Even though the invitation was a week and a half in advance of the date, we already had plans.

"Thanks, but we're going out of town that weekend. Maybe some other night?" I asked my son.

"Well, uh, OK," he said.

Justin didn't sound exactly enthusiastic about my answer. I chalked up his reaction to the state of his job. Lately it had been driving him crazy. He really didn't need a night of playing host to his parents. Going out with friends would be much more relaxing for him. I didn't give the matter further thought and never even mentioned it to my husband, Phil.

The next day, Justin called me again.

"We really want you to come to dinner."

"Justin, I told you we're going out of town. We can come

some other night."

"I know, but things are really hectic and the only night we can get together is Saturday. We need to see you . . . we have a big announcement to make."

My body came to attention like a bird dog on point.

"What kind of announcement?"

"We'll tell you at dinner. See you then."

The call disconnected.

I hustled over to the couch where Phil lounged, watching television.

"Justin says we have to come to his house a week from Saturday for dinner. They have a big announcement!"

He frowned, and his words dripped with finality. "We're going out of town."

"Oh no, we're not. I'm not going to miss any big announcement. I'll bet he and Kathy finally got engaged!"

I'd been hoping for them to make it official for months. I had even stooped to dropping a few hints to Justin about jewelry store sales.

Phil simply rolled his eyes at my conclusion and sighed. "Fine. We'll cancel our weekend. But I think you're making way too much out of this. He probably got a promotion at work or something."

Did I mention that my husband isn't very intuitive in matters of love? I went into the other room to turn on a wedding-planner television show and began to dream about fluffy white dresses and tailored black tuxedos.

The next day I called our daughter Jessica and told her about the dinner date with Justin and Kathy. After gushing about how I couldn't wait to see the engagement ring, she interrupted me.

"Mom, I don't think that's it at all. He told me he had interviews for a new job that's out of town. I'll bet he got the job, and they have to relocate."

My eyes widened. I hadn't even considered anything like that. Nor did I care to.

Three days later, I spent an evening with one of my best friends and couldn't resist venting. I told her what Jessica said then reiterated my own theory about a wedding, waiting for some reassurance. Her tone sounded annoyingly nonchalant.

"Who knows what he'll say? You never can tell with kids."

*So much for counting on the support of friends,* I told myself. No one seemed to understand how I felt.

On the afternoon of our dinner with Justin and Kathy, I got dressed and brushed my hair. I felt a mixture of excitement and fear. There were plenty of possibilities on what the evening might bring. I doggedly hoped for the best one.

Soon we got into our car and headed to Justin's house. Along the way, I tried to convince Phil—and myself—that my theory of an engagement would happen that evening. Surely, with any other type of news, Justin wouldn't keep us in suspense. Besides, he wouldn't want to move away. He'd put too much work into his house lately. An ominous new thought emerged: *What if selling his house could be the reason for all the work he'd done on it?* I shut my mouth, turned up the radio and tried to breathe.

We pulled into Justin's neighborhood and drove down streets lined by beautiful and well-kept homes. I could hear my heart pounding in my ears nearly as loudly as the music from the radio. Our car rounded a wide left turn that would put us directly in front of his house.

When we came around the bend, I couldn't see his yard for the dozens of people standing in it. Cars were parked on both sides of the street. *He must have invited all his friends. What in the world kind of announcement did he have in mind?*

Then I recognized faces. They weren't Justin's friends— they were our friends' faces. And there stood our daughter, sisters, brothers, nieces and nephews.

Phil stopped the car and we looked at each other with mouths agape. I swallowed and spoke first. "Our anniversary!"

I'd been so wrapped up in Justin's big announcement that I'd forgotten all about our 35th wedding anniversary. A chorus of voices shouted, "Surprise!" as we exited the car. Never had I felt quite so clueless. Pulling off a surprise party is a challenge, but our son and daughter managed to prove that it's easy to fool a couple of old fools.

Once the shock had subsided, the food had disappeared and all the old stories had been told, our surprise anniversary party came to an end. After the final guest departed, I tracked down Justin and gave him a hug. He apologized for the comment that he knew would lead me to my own set of conclusions.

"Jessica and I figured telling you that would be the only way we could get you here for sure, Mom."

I laughed at his accurate, if unflattering, observation and poked his arm with my finger. "Just so you know, mister, as far as I'm concerned, you still owe me a big announcement."

And guess what? I finally got it. Justin and Kathy are now planning their wedding. Which goes to show that sometimes if you are patient enough, you will finally hear the big announcement you've been waiting for—even if you have to cash in an I.O.U. from your son to get it.

Pat with husband Phil cutting their surprise anniversary cake

Pat (right) finally cashed in on her I.O.U from Justin (left). He married Kathy in September 2012

# An Almost Perfect Lady

by
Morton Levy

Most of the time, my maternal grandmother, Bessie Moss, was a lady. So was my dad's mom, Helen Greenfield. They were very formal when they spoke, calling each other "Mrs. Moss" and "Mrs. Greenfield." And when they spoke of their friends, they did so in a similar fashion. These two fine ladies never went out in public without hats, and even when they went shopping or out to tea, they wore short white gloves.

Both had immigrated to the United States as children in the 1880s, and neither came from wealthy or sophisticated families. They did not have a great deal of formal education. Their attempt to be ladies was just one of their attempts to behave in a fashion that they felt would make them Americans.

On Saturdays, Grandma Moss would take me to movies or shopping downtown. One Saturday when I was seven years old, my gentle, well-mannered grandmother and I were, as was often the case, riding downtown from the Delmar Loop in what was called a "service car" in St. Louis—or a "jitney" in other places. This was a more fashionable mode of transportation as compared to a streetcar, and since the ride cost only 25 cents instead of a dime, my grandmother found it to be a cheap way to move up in social status.

On this particular Saturday during our ride, Grandma Moss observed a woman walking down the sidewalk and declared with firm resolution, "That lady ought to sue the city."

"Why, Grandma?" I asked.

"For building the sidewalk too close to her ass."

Everyone in the car laughed, but I didn't understand what was so funny. I wanted an explanation, but was too shy to ask at the time. When I got home that afternoon, I went to find my mother to see if she could tell me what it all meant.

"What's an 'ass'?" I asked.

"Why do you want to know?"

"Well, Grandma said this lady we saw could sue the city for building the sidewalk too close to her ass. Everybody in the service car laughed, but I didn't understand what was so funny."

"It is a nasty word for 'rear end' or 'fanny,'" Mom replied.

"Does the city really measure people before they build a sidewalk?" was my next question.

"No. It's just a way of saying that someone is short and fat," she advised.

Now I was really confused. I couldn't understand why my grandmother would say such a thing. Not because it was nasty or mean, even though it was both. It was because my grandmother was only 4 feet 11 inches tall and weighed close to 200 pounds.

Though I never forgot the incident, I was not ever able to bring that question up to her. It was clearly a sign that my Grandma Bessie, in addition to being a loving soul, also had a dark side.

When I was a teenager, I discovered she enjoyed gambling. Once she and my dad's mother, my Grandma Greenfield—I never called her "Helen"—disappeared for a whole afternoon. They each had taken a streetcar downtown and were supposed to meet for lunch before doing some shopping.

When neither had come home by five o'clock, my mom and my dad's sister—my Aunt Hennie—were on the phone, sharing each other's panic. By six, there was even greater anxiety. My mom asked our next-door neighbor, who was the chief of police, what she should do. He urged patience.

Mom called Aunt Hennie and told her to stay calm, even though she was clearly a nervous wreck herself. Then to keep busy, Mom went about the routine of fixing an overdue dinner.

At 6:30 P.M., a Yellow Cab pulled up in front of our house. From my watch post in the bay window of my second-floor bedroom, I saw my 78-year-old grandmother bounce out of the car and walk up the stairs that traversed our steeply terraced front lawn with more speed than I had ever seen her produce. I shouted, "She's home!" and ran downstairs.

As Grandma came through the door, my mother shouted at her, "Where have you been?! We were worried sick!" The phone rang, sparing us all more yelling. Mom answered and returned saying, "That was Henrietta, letting me know Mrs. Greenfield was safe at home. Where were the two of you?"

"Shopping was boring. We each bought a few things then

we caught a cab and went to Burns' Steak House across the river—a fine dining establishment with a horse parlor upstairs—to play the horses."

"You did what?!" Mom exclaimed.

"We each won $60, that's what we did."

Then she reached in her purse, pulled out two silver dollars and handed them to me, adding, "We were doing so good, we didn't want to miss the last race."

Grandma Bessie lived in the same house as I did until she was 85. At times, I related to her as a second mother. In spite of her indiscretions, I loved her, respected her and thought of her as a lady in the strictest sense.

Most of the time.

Grandma Helen Greenfield (left) and Grandma Bessie Moss

# The Family that Votes Together . . .

by
Frank Ramirez

On a November morning in the year 2000, my family and I sat in a restaurant, waiting for the sun to rise in that cold hour before dawn. We complained about the coffee and fiddled with our eggs, which didn't look nearly as appetizing as they did on the glossy menu. It was at that moment two things became perfectly obvious to me.

First, no one in the Ramirez family does mornings well. We're grouchy, out of sorts and always ready to press the snooze button so we can roll over and go back to sleep. But we'd had important business that morning and we'd already accomplished it.

And second, on that particular day, for the first time ever, all five of us were eligible to vote in the presidential election. And we had all voted the same.

Polls open at 6 A.M. in the state of Indiana and they close 12 hours later. Maybe it's because Indiana is an agricultural state, so Hoosiers rise with the sun and sleep when it gets dark. Our oldest son Francisco and our daughter Jessica both attended Manchester College, a little over an hour from our home in rural northern Indiana, about halfway between Elkhart and Goshen. Our youngest son Jacob was still in high school, but he had turned 18 only a few days before and had registered in time to vote. For all three, it was their first time to cast a presidential ballot.

The two college students had come home to spend the night so we could all vote together as a family, after which they'd rush back to campus for class. We'd turned the event into a slumber party, complete with popcorn, movies and a late bedtime that made little sense once the alarm clocks went off that morning.

My wife Jennie and I don't force our views on anyone, although we're always ready to defend our way of thinking. This was especially true with regards to our children. We wanted them to think for themselves, make up their own minds and chart their own courses. At least that's what we said aloud. But deep inside, we were hoping they'd grow up to think a lot like us.

And that includes voting Democrat. We're California natives, a blue state that's pretty schizophrenic, veering toward the red and infrared before turning ultraviolet. California Democrats—and to be fair, Republicans, as well—are independent thinkers, and we're not comfortable with having to toe a party line.

Values are values. However, the way we instilled them was by example rather than words. When I was pastor at a multiracial church in Los Angeles, our kids learned by our example that that racism isn't just wrong—it's stupid. We cared for those on the margins of society—the weak, the poor, senior citizens, children. The kids saw us take care of folks who dropped by the parsonage hoping for something to eat, or rushing out in the middle of the night to provide care for those who were hurting.

And we showed them we considered voting very important by never missing an election. When they were young, we took them with us into the voting booth.

Things didn't change when we moved to a new church in Indiana. The country-church congregation was all white and rural, and when we partnered with the local African Methodist Episcopal congregation to offer joint Bible studies and vacation Bible schools, many were excited about taking part. But others disagreed so strongly they worked behind the scenes against this partnership. Our kids loved what we were doing, but they were aware of the opposition, too.

But how would this translate when it came to adulthood? Preaching at someone rarely works. That's why, despite our titles, we preachers rarely preach at people. We serve them.

Come the teen years, our kids rebelled like everyone else's. Francisco was the expert at music, food, travel and theater and was always at the center of every circle. Jessica was not flashy. She was a perfectionist who worked hard to accomplish everything in school and was recognized as competent by all who knew her. Jacob—hilariously funny, quick-witted, sharp and bright—overcame his attention deficit disorder and eventually graduated from college like his older brother and sister. We thought the world of them, but what did they—as teenagers—think of us? Not much, evidently.

But I'm the patient kind. And then it happened. Our daughter and my wife had been arguing, as daughters and mothers do, and were hardly speaking. But I was standing behind Jessica while she went through Jennie's line where she worked as a grocery-store clerk. And though they hadn't planned it, they were wearing the same "Fight Racism" buttons. Maybe we'd been good parents after all.

So, on Election Day 2000, with George W. Bush and Al Gore competing against one another for the President of the United States, we were pretty much the first ones to vote. We didn't want to wait in a long line, not with a 70-minute drive ahead of us to get the older two off to class on time. When the doors to our polling place opened, we stepped through from darkness and cold into light.

In Indiana, judges from the two major parties are required to sit together at tables and monitor the election. It's a small town and everyone knew who we were and how we would vote. We signed the registers, got our ballots and punched our choices clean through. No one had heard of "hanging chads"—not until later in that very same election.

Some might have said we'd wasted our votes in a state that was bound to go Republican, but we knew better. Never mind about coffee or breakfast. Never mind that it was way too early. We'd done something that really mattered, and with no coercion or pressure from Jennie or me, we'd shown that values can be passed on to our children.

The family that votes together sticks together. No, it doesn't rhyme, but it doesn't have to. It just has to be true.

The Ramirez family (l to r) Jennie, Jacob, Jessica, Frank and Francisco

# Blended

by
Margaret Lalich

I love the 007 character in the *James Bond* series. I always thought his ultrasuave and worldly manner was beautifully illustrated whenever he ordered a martini. He'd request it "shaken—not stirred" to avoid bruising the gin.

As a single mother of two boys, I have tried to be suave and blend in with the world around me, but with much less success than 007. Of course, Bond relied on a well-written script and a director to help him keep the right balance of action and cool. My life has been a more spontaneous production, and "cool" has been occasionally hard to come by.

It was just eight weeks before my second wedding. This marriage would create a blended family for my boys—ages seven and nine—and my fiancé's girls, who were older. My fiancé and I had worked together for many years, and my sons had known him since their diaper days. With affection, they had tagged him "Uncle Joe." He wore that title proudly for the six years it took romance to advance to engagement and then marriage.

For all of those years up to our marriage, we had been a trio—just me and my boys. Desiring that our impending nuptials be as anxiety-free as possible for all of us, I seriously wanted to be as warm and as wise and as suave as James Bond in preparing them for the big change. I didn't know what to expect.

The night finally came for my sit-down, heart-to-heart conversation with my sons about the change in our family status after the marriage took place. I prepared for this conversation with much prayer, meditation and, of course, lots of hot chocolate all around.

After going through my somewhat-prepared speech, the boys were very quiet and serious as they considered the proposal. They both told me they were happy with the idea of having more time with the man who had become their hero. Picnic-bag races, Boy Scouts' pinewood derby construction, mastery of the softball pitch and the art of self-defense were all familiar territory for my boys and their Uncle Joe. But I knew that having Uncle Joe around full time would be different for them both.

But I didn't have to worry—too much. One of them asked me, "If *we're* gonna get married, can we call him 'Dad'?" With all the bravado and coolness I could muster—aka 007—I answered that they certainly could, but they didn't have to. They both smiled.

Then my youngest changed the subject. His mechanical bank, which he was holding, was broken and he wasn't sure he could fix it. Working on the coin bank with serious concentration didn't help. He grimaced and his body slumped as he gave up his efforts to repair it. Suddenly, he shot back up, filled with hope. Face aglow, he said, "Hey, I can ask *Uncle* Dad to fix it!"

Bond's quote came to mind: "Shaken—not stirred." We were blending, not bruising!

# Foolish Kisses

by
## Pat Nelson

My parents were already old, in their 30s, when I was born. As a teenager, it had embarrassed me to have older parents. I had been glad they didn't hold hands or kiss. It would have been unbearable.

It shouldn't have surprised me that my parents didn't display affection. "Gram"—Mom's mom—was known for her no-nonsense, stern demeanor. She never put up with any funny business.

On my dad's side of the family, when he was only seven years old, his father ran off, leaving his mother to raise the children alone on a soggy, mosquito-infested piece of swampland in Northern Minnesota. Hard work and poor conditions took their toll, and she died when Dad was only 13.

There were lots of kids in his family. Dad always said there were eight in the first litter and seven in the second. Considering there were so many kids, my paternal grandparents must have had more than a few intimate moments. But I learned that they never hugged or kissed in front of their children. For this reason, my dad, too, had missed out on witnessing warm displays of affection.

In 1957, we got our first TV. I remember sitting in front of the new box that would expand my world, excitedly searching the snow on the screen for recognizable images. Once the rabbit ears were in place and a signal had been captured, I curiously watched TV families who ever so discretely displayed more affection than I had ever seen in my family. If a kiss on a TV show was more than just a quick peck on the cheek, Mom complained about all that mushiness or just plain foolishness. Daddy didn't say anything.

As a teenager, I experimented with kissing, and it didn't seem so bad. In fact, I kind of enjoyed it. My best friend and I kept a list of all the boys we kissed, carving their names inside the wooden door of my armoire. Our parents would have died if they had known it was a list of our mushy and foolish actions.

In my family, we weren't much on saying, "I love you," although we truly did love each other. There's a joke that goes like this: "Did you hear about the Norwegian man who loved his wife so much he almost told her?" Well, our family had enough Norwegian in it to follow that practice. That unspoken rule caused me deep regret when Dad lay in his hospital bed, brain dead. I realized I had never told him I loved him. I took his cold, unresponsive hand in my warm hands and hot tears poured out my loss as I squeaked out a barely-audible, "I love you."

As a mother, I was more affectionate than my parents had ever been, possibly because I'd been influenced by television.

Besides, I grew up in the liberal 1960s, and those in my generation thought we had invented affection.

When my best friend's mother died, my mother—who was a widow—and my friend's widower father started to spend time together. We didn't think much about these two lonely old friends going to dinner together, and it took me a while to realize that these outings were actually dates. The idea of my mother dating was almost inconceivable.

Next, they began traveling together, even sharing a motel room to stretch their Social Security income. After one of those trips, they came to our house to tell us about their adventure. My husband brought extra chairs into the living room so everyone could be seated. Instead of sitting on her own chair, my 70-year-old mother scooted up onto her date's lap. She placed her arm around his neck as though it wasn't the first time she had done so, and he affectionately wrapped his arms around her. I watched my kids exchange shocked glances. I tried to look nonchalant. "So," I said, "tell us about your trip."

Mom had a new sparkle in her eyes. She giggled and the two of them made eye contact as they told their story. *Do they even know we're in the room?* I wondered. Mom's boyfriend seemed to be all she could think about. *Weird, just plain weird,* I thought. *Why is she acting so foolish?*

They finished recounting the story of their travels, and Mom said enthusiastically, "I had such a good time!" That's when she planted a big, loud kiss on her boyfriend's lips.

My face turned red with embarrassment as I wondered, *Why all this foolish mushiness?* Then I realized that it's never too late for planting affection.

# Telltale Possessions

by
Janet Sheppard Kelleher

I'm a dust-catcher collector.

There, I admitted it. I've had this disease so long that I learned early in our marriage to pack some sentimental possessions periodically and store them in the attic to make room for new ones. Consequently, some things are rediscovered that have not seen the light of day for several years. Such was the case of one item.

Uncharacteristically quiet that day, Jillie, our youngest at eight, seemed to be mulling over something. I figured it would surface eventually and she'd talk about it.

Sure enough, when dinner rolled around that evening, Jillie was observant, but not contributing anything to the conversation. Normally exuberant, she sulked and contemplated. I could see her wheels turning like she was grinding grits. Something was on her mind.

During a lull in the conversation, she looked rather

peaked, despondent even. She stared at her dad a long time. A LONG TIME. She gave him the evil eye. Then she finally broke her gaze and pushed her little cherub face up to mine and demanded, "Mommy, who's my real daddy?"

I examined her dad's face. He rolled his eyes and shook his head. I searched her brother's face. At 16, he smirked and shrugged his slouching shoulders. I inspected her sister's face. At 12, she just giggled as if Jillie had unearthed some juicy family secret of which she would soon be privy.

I looked back at my baby girl and caressed her cheek. "What do you mean, sweetie? Daddy is your real daddy."

Jillie pursed her lips like Shirley Temple and argued, "No, no, no! I mean that first man you married!"

My husband Irish and I looked at one another without an answer. Neither he nor I had been married before. Dumb-founded, I again asked, "What do you mean, darling? Daddy and I have only been married to each other. He's David's daddy and Sarah's daddy. And he's your daddy, too!"

That answer still didn't satisfy Jillie. She left the table, ran to the den and came back lugging our wedding portrait, one I had pulled from the attic and placed on the shelf while she was at school that day. It hadn't been on the shelves since Jillie had been old enough to remember.

"This man, Mommy! Who is this man?!"

Even her dad—bless his slandered heart—admitted that he lacked the thin frame and dark hair of the man I'd married. During my first pregnancy he gained 30 pounds. Only he didn't nurse the baby and he didn't lose the weight. Similarly, he gained more with the second pregnancy and even more during my pregnancy with Jillie.

In 18 years, Jillie's daddy had become quite chunky and had made strides in the prematurely-gray department. In eight short years of living, Jillie had only known the stout man with the white mustache who looked like Captain Kangaroo.

Life is what it is. And it changes us . . . for better or worse. I am now one self-confessed dust-catcher collector who has changed her ways—I am much more selective in culling future heirlooms and telltale possessions.

Wedding day for
Janet and Irish

Irish, 18 years later

# Pigs in Blankets

by
## Paprika Furstenberg

Childhood is a time to learn skills we'll need for the rest of our lives. Sharing, turn-taking and responsibility come to mind, but giving a child a designated bedtime offers that child the opportunity to develop negotiating skills.

Bargaining to stay up past a set bedtime is a rite of passage. As a child, I learned and exploited variables that affected my negotiations. It was important to know my audience—cajoling a baby sitter or grandparent to let me stay up late was always easier than trying the same trick on my parents.

My negotiating tactics were more effective during vacations than on school nights. But the most difficult bedtime negotiations occurred when I tried to convince my parents to let me stay up until midnight on New Year's Eve. I had a persuasive argument—it wasn't a school night and everyone else in the world was doing it.

When I was in elementary school, New Year's Eve looked

like so much fun. There were confetti, party hats, noisemakers and hors d'oeuvres, all at a time of day I rarely got to experience. It was magical!

Finally, when winter break from school began, so, too, did my plan to stay up until midnight on New Year's Eve. I was on my best behavior, offered to do all sorts of chores for no additional allowance and was even nice to my younger brother.

After an exhausting week of stellar behavior, the next step—the negotiations—began in earnest. To my great surprise, my parents agreed to let my brother and me stay up until midnight, as long as we promised to be in bed by 12:30 A.M. It was a deal. We were so excited! My mom got us party hats, really loud noisemakers and even bought a box of frozen, "fancy" hors d'oeuvres just for the two of us—pigs in blankets.

In the 1970s, before every appliance in the house had a digital clock, we had a grandfather clock in the living room. It was a huge clock that chimed the hours of the day. No matter where you were in the house, you could hear the bonging of those bells.

When December 31st arrived, we listened to the grandfather clock tick away the hours until midnight. Our excitement grew. Our mouths watered at the idea of eating tiny hot dogs wrapped in buttery dough at a time when we would have normally been asleep. When the clock finally struck 12, we all shouted, "Happy New Year!" and waved our noisemakers around and stuffed our faces with greasy snacks. At 12:30, my brother and I went to our rooms without argument and fell asleep like all good children do.

Many years later, after I was married, I told my husband the story of my childhood New Year's Eve negotiation triumph over my parents, and how staying up on that day became a family tradition. Since it happened to be on New Year's Eve when I shared the story, I made us pigs in blankets to celebrate.

The next day, I called my parents to wish them a Happy New Year. My dad answered the phone and asked me what we had done to celebrate the night before. I told him we had a quiet evening at home, eating traditional pigs in blankets.

"Traditional pigs in blankets?" he asked.

"Yes. Don't you remember? In elementary school, you let us stay up past our bedtime on New Year's Eve. We always had pigs in blankets around midnight. It's one of my favorite childhood memories."

"I have something to tell you," Dad said tentatively. "You did eat pigs in blankets, but you never stayed up until midnight."

"What do you mean? I distinctly remember the big clock chiming 12 times. I remember sitting on the floor in front of it, waiting for the two hands to reach the 12." I was confused.

"The clock did strike 12, but it was really 10 o'clock. We knew you could tell time, so we couldn't lie to you about what time was on the clock. While you were busy playing, we turned the clock ahead two hours," Dad explained, laughing as he did so.

"So all those years, I thought I was ringing in the New Year when I was actually celebrating the final two hours of the old year?!" I was stunned at this news. My confidence in my negotiating skills had been shattered.

"Yes," he said, without a shred of remorse.

"You only did this once, right?" I asked, but was afraid of the response.

"No, we did this until you were almost a teenager." He sounded quite pleased with himself.

"Years?! You perpetrated this fraud on your own child for years?! And you're just telling me now?!" I couldn't believe what I was hearing. It was bad enough to think I had been fooled once, but to learn that I had been bamboozled all those years was astounding.

"Don't you feel even a little bit guilty for tricking me for all those years, Dad?"

There was a long pause. "Nope, I don't feel guilty at all. In fact, I think it was quite clever. You thought you were staying up late, and we didn't have to listen to any bargaining or whining. Plus, once you and your brother went to bed, your mom and I got to have a peaceful New Year's Eve. It was a win-win situation." I could just imagine the impish grin on his face while telling me this.

Now I'm older and hopefully a bit wiser. The jury is out as to whether or not my negotiating skills have improved. I have reached the age when staying up until midnight to ring in the New Year is not a novelty. In fact, some years my husband and I have even fallen asleep before midnight, but it was always with a tummy full of pigs in blankets.

# CHAPTER EIGHT

# All in the Family

Family fun at its finest!

# Farmer on the Dell

by
Melissa Face

"I'll call you back in 10 minutes," my mom promised. "I have to go harvest my crops."

Perhaps you are picturing my mother, a woman in her late 50s, atop an International tractor, plowing a field. Dressed in a plaid shirt and coveralls, she's also wearing a straw hat to protect her from the sweltering Virginia sun.

That is definitely the wrong picture.

My mom farms from a pink Dell laptop. She farms in good weather and bad, during the summer and the winter, at home and on vacation. She can fertilize and plow from any place with Internet access. She is a *Farmville* farmer.

Mom opened a Facebook account a few years ago and began playing *Farmville* not too long after. She tried really hard to get me interested in the game. She spoke of barn raisings and vineyards and orchards. She tried to entice me with country collectibles, rare chickens and bushels of raspberries. There were times when I considered joining her on the farm, but I knew I already spent too much time on the Internet. I didn't need something else to check each day.

As time passed, Mom started expanding her farm. She built French cottages, added new pastures and planted rows of trees. Her farm required more and more of her time. And she managed it quite nicely.

Last spring, she made arrangements when she knew we would be traveling to the beach. "I'm only planting half the crops I usually do," she said. "That way I won't have to worry about harvesting when we're gone."

Mom enjoyed her vacation. We all went shopping during the day and ate dinner together each evening. But at night, when everyone else was heading for bed, Mom went upstairs, turned on her Dell and checked on her farm.

"Three little lambs were born last night," she announced during breakfast. "I gave them really cute names, too. One of them is called 'Ram Bunctious.'"

The next night, my husband and I were awakened by a strange noise. At first, we thought the baby was crying. We soon realized we were hearing cows mooing, sheep bleating and pigs oinking. Mom was working on her farm and she had forgotten to turn down the volume on her computer. Unfortunately, sleep is sometimes sacrificed when your mother is a farmer.

I call my mom in the afternoons when I am on my way home from work. It is the one time of day when I know we can chat about work, family and our favorite TV shows without being interrupted. Occasionally, though, Mom's voice will trail off or she will answer a question that I asked much earlier in the conversation. Then I hear her mouse clicking in the background and I realize she is farming.

"I'll call you back later," I tell her.

"I was just collecting some eggs," she says.

"I'll call you after I pick up the baby," I say.

"There. I'm done. I'm signing off now. What were you saying?" she asks.

We all give Mom a hard time about her *Farmville*. We laugh at her mystery trees, joke about her ducklings and make snide remarks about her pigpens. My dad tells her it's ridiculous. I tell her she's addicted. But she keeps playing and so do all of her *Farmville* friends.

And why shouldn't she? It's free and apparently a great deal of fun. My mom deserves to have fun now that she is semi-retired. And it really doesn't cause any major problems, aside from some overcrowding I noticed in one of her chicken coops. But she worked on that situation after I threatened to contact PETA.

I was planning on calling my mom this afternoon before the hectic workweek begins. But according to her online status, she is already working—in her horse stables. I guess if I

want to talk with her more, I'm going to have to join her. Maybe I will go ahead and start my own farm this summer. After all, farming is a family industry. And I already have my own Dell.

Mom (Kim) and Melissa

# You Bet Your M&M's!

by
Norine Dworkin-McDaniel

We recently marked a milestone in our house. We quietly and surreptitiously retired the board game Candy Land.

I don't say "quietly" and "surreptitiously" because I enjoy hiding toys from my kid. No—I just didn't want to do anything that might alert my little hoarder-in-training that the game had gone missing. Fletcher is a kid who would stash away every plaything he's ever had since babyhood if our house had enough closets. If you've ever attempted a toy purge in the presence of a child, you know it's not pleasant. Even if he's never so much as touched that $80 workbench you bought because he was enthralled with Daddy's tools, he'll fight to keep it. The mere threat that it might leave the house f-o-r-e-v-e-r will prompt him to cling, sobbing, to that molded plastic like an environmental activist chained to a tree. Said sobbing will cease only when you return the item to the playroom where it will sit untouched until the next purge.

I now do all toy purging on the sly. Candy Land was purged because it was excruciatingly dull. If you haven't gotten to this particular stage of parenthood yet, here's a friendly heads-up: Candy Land is the tranquilizer of board games. Go ahead and play a few rounds the next time you can't fall asleep—it works better than Valium. Mid-game, you could probably drill my teeth and I wouldn't flinch.

Yes, I understood the game's developmental value for in-troducing tots to structured game play—and for teaching how not to hurl pieces at the wall and stomp on the board when you lose, though we're still waiting for that particular lesson to sink in at our home. But spend a few years pushing a plastic gingerbread man through a junk-food forest, from red space to blue space to green space to orange space, and your brain will feel about as sharp as those beginner knives you find in toddler cutlery sets. After a couple of hours on a rainy Satur-day, you'll beg to stop playing. You'll barter a kidney to stop playing. Because, as anyone who has ever gotten within strik-ing distance of that "Promised Land o' Sweets" only to draw the dreaded Gingerbread Man card and be booted back to the beginning knows, the game never stops. It's like pedaling a sta-tionary bike. You could play forever and never get there. In fact, I think we were still in the middle of the first game we started when we opened the box three years ago. Deep-sixing this baby wasn't mean—it was self-preservation.

So, with Candy Land hidden away on the top shelf in the back corner of my office closet, I was free to introduce Fletch-er to games that I wouldn't need a double Scotch (or several) to endure. Games like Othello, Sorry and Chinese checkers.

Eventually, I figured, we'd graduate to Mastermind, Scrabble and my personal favorite, Stratego. In my daydreams, I envisioned our little family gathered, Norman Rockwell-style, around the table for family game night with a big bowl of popcorn, our Golden Retriever happily resting at our feet and a nice cozy fire in the fireplace. OK, so we don't have a fireplace. Or a dog. I'm actually more of a cat person. But you get the picture of the wholesome Hallmark Channel-kind of family fun I had in mind.

So when it was time for Family Game Night, do you know what my sweet, pink-cheeked little cherub wanted to play instead? Poker. Yes sir, that's my baby—the budding card shark.

I've asked Fletcher repeatedly and still don't know what put the idea into his head, where he even heard about poker. It's not like my husband, Stewart, has a weekly poker game. No one we know plays poker. My parents occasionally talk about "bridge," but as far as Fletcher's concerned, they're discussing a crumbling infrastructure in London, not cards. I spent four years in Vegas and still can't tell the difference between a straight and a flush. To me, a full house means having weekend guests.

Of course, I was grateful that my boy wasn't clamoring for Candy Land. But, seriously, in what universe is poker an appropriate game for a five-year-old?

"Is gambling really the best example to set for our child?" I asked Stewart when he agreed to teach our son Texas Hold 'Em. Stewart shrugged off my concerns in the way that husbands the world over shrug off their wives' concerns when they think we're overreacting.

My mind raced. *What's next? Blackjack? Showing him how*

*to blow smoke rings? Mix martinis?* I anticipated a summons from his Montessori-school teacher: "Fletcher's reading well and starting to master subtraction. But we are concerned that he's hustling poker games on the playground. Please see me at your earliest convenience." And I knew when they gave out Debauched Parents of the Year awards, we would be shoo-ins for the Under Six category.

But Stewart pointed out to me that we had already exposed Fletcher to gambling by playing dreidel during Hanukkah. If you've never played, dreidel is like rudimentary craps, but rather than rolling dice, you spin a top with Hebrew letters on it then put pennies into a pot or take them out based on which letter comes up. It's a children's game. But there's probably a bookie who takes odds on it somewhere.

"Hon, we're not talking about roulette or throwing dice," Stewart said, still trying to win me over. "Poker's a sophisticated game of skill."

*Yeah, yeah. You say "po-TAY-toe."* I thought. I worried Child Services would be banging on our door at any moment. But I knew I wasn't going to win this one. I found myself caught between a child who has raised relentless pleading to an art form and a husband who had logged his share of glassy-eyed hours on Candy Land duty and was equally desperate for more stimulating diversions,

"All right, all right. We'll play. But no cash. We'll use M&M's." My two boys happily agreed.

*At least I'd drawn a line somewhere.* Though, on reflection, I realized that in future years Fletcher would be able to tell his therapist how his parents set him up for gambling addiction *and* diabetes. It was too late to buy back on that one though. Fletcher was already rummaging in the pantry for his Halloween stash.

"Found the M&M's, Mommy!"

*Oh goody.*

I wondered if maybe, between the anteing up, the calling and the raising, we could consider poker a "math exercise." Oh yeah, I was grasping. That's a whopper of a rationalization. But I figured it was my best defense if Child Services came calling.

So our traditional "Family Game Night" became "Hold 'Em Night." Stewart outlined the basics of our sophisticated game of skill . . . er, math. He explained "the flop," "the turn" and "the river." He detailed the different types of winning hands and what it meant to check, to call, to raise and to match a bet to "make the pot right."

*OK, there was some addition. Maybe calling this a math exercise wasn't such a stretch after all.*

At first, we played our cards face up so Fletcher could get the hang of putting together two-of-a-kind, three-of-a-kind, four-of-a-kind, flushes and straights from the cards he held and the community cards on the table.

"How's that for some set theory?" Stewart asked me, pointedly. *More math. Sweet.*

Then we were ready to play for real.

We tossed M&M's into the pot, and Stewart dealt the cards. Two to each of us and three face down in the middle—the flop.

"I dealt, so it's your bet, Fletcher," Stewart said, nodding at him.

Fletcher knocked his little fist on the table. "Check," he said. "I wanna see it for free." One lesson and he'd already gotten the lingo down.

I checked and Stewart checked. Then Stewart flipped the three community cards over: before us was an ace of hearts, five of spades and 10 of clubs. This did nothing to help the cards in my hand. But Fletcher gave a little squeal and with a big grin, he pushed a bunch of his candy into the pot.

"Ooooh, Maaaah-mee," he taunted, through a mouthful of chocolate. "I'm gonna beat you. I'm gonna beat you."

"OK, Poker Face," I tousled his hair. "Try to save some chocolate for the game."

"Here comes the turn." Stewart dealt the fourth card, the 10 of diamonds. "Everyone's got a pair of 10s. Fletcher, your bet."

Fletcher pushed more of his candy into the pot. "I've got the best hand! I'm gonna beat you. I've got the best hand. I'm gonna beat you," he chanted, dancing excitedly in his seat. "I'm gonna take you to the laundry."

"To the cleaners, baby," I laughed. "You're going to take us to the cleaners." So he didn't have all the lingo down yet.

"Uh-huh. Can I show you? Can I show you?"

"Not yet. Let's wait for the last card," I said. Even though I had nothing besides the pair of 10s showing on the table, I tossed more M&M's into the pot anyway.

"And the river," Stewart said as he laid down the last card, the queen of hearts. "OK, Fletcher. Whaddya wanna do?"

"All in!" Fletcher pushed the rest of his candy into the center of the table. "Can I show you now?

We'd noticed during practice play that Fletcher loved

to bet heavy—more because he enjoyed seeing a big pile of candy on the table rather than any real understanding of how to bluff. So wagering his sizeable pile of M&M's could mean he had pocket aces or nothing at all. And I didn't want game night to end with him sulking, face down in the couch cushions because he'd lost all his chocolate.

"You really want to bet all your candy?" I asked gently. He nodded, fiercely.

"All right," I said. Both Stewart and I added the rest of our M&M's to the pile, too. We were all in.

"Turn 'em over," Stewart said to Fletcher.

Fletcher gleefully turned over his cards. It took a full moment to register. Then Stewart and I looked at each other in disbelief. There on the table, between the community cards and his own, was a pair of aces and three 10s.

The kid had a full house.

*Seriously. What are the odds?* I wondered. Stewart and I looked at the cards then at each other, sharing a bewildered and bemused "how-the- f_ _ k-did-that-happen?!" look.

"Mommy, Daddy, I told you I would win," Fletcher said confidently through the melted chocolate smeared on his face.

*Forget Candy Land. Score one for poker math,* I thought. Then I brushed the chocolate off my little card shark's teeth and tucked him into bed.

# Would It Kill Ya?

by
## Stacey Gustafson

Don't get me wrong—I love being a stay-at-home mom. With a smile, I'll do laundry, prepare meals, vacuum and even pick up you-know-what after the dog. But would it kill the rest of my family to help with household chores without all the whining?

One morning, my high-school-aged daughter tapped a pencil 15 times on the kitchen counter, sighed and gripped her cellphone tight enough to lose circulation. This was her signal that she was ready to leave for school.

"Let's go, Mom," she said, while finishing a text message. "My friends are waiting."

I scanned the kitchen and spied her half-finished glass of orange juice, crusty bowl of cereal and crushed napkin near her placemat on the table.

"Please pick up your mess," I said, wiping the counter with a dishrag.

My daughter remained motionless, except for her thumbs.

"Come on, Mom. We're late."

"Would it kill ya to put the dishes in the sink?" I asked, rubbing the back of my neck.

"What's the big deal?"

Back home, I poured a cup of Joe and relaxed for 20 minutes—but it only felt like 10 seconds. I peeked at the clock and realized that if my 13-year-old son didn't clean up, pack up and hurry up, he'd be late for first period.

"Time to go," I uttered and grabbed the car keys. "Get your homework and meet me at the car."

I watched from the driver's seat as my boy exited the back-door and ambled down the driveway, sluggish and drowsy, as though wading through Jell-O. With droopy drawers and downcast eyes, he dragged his feet the entire distance. I averted my eyes and laughed a little to myself. *How is it possible to move that slowly?* I thought. Earlier, he was riding his scooter and shooting basketball hoops at the same time.

"Would it kill ya to walk any faster?!" I cried out the window, placing my head on the steering wheel in mock frustration.

"I'm hurrying. Be right there."

"You're going to be late."

"Chill."

My expectations for my family were simple. Would it kill anyone to place scissors back in the drawer after using them? Put their shoes in the correct spot? Hang up a jacket? Be on time? *Am I asking too much?*

At dinnertime, I tried to squeeze out help with the evening chores. I craved spending quiet time with my husband before he dozed off on the sofa. If everyone pitched in, I wouldn't be stuck doing everything and we could all relax and unwind.

"Honey, please clear the table," I said to my son.

"Can you do it? I gotta go," he said, dodging eye contact.

"Go where?"

He tilted his head in the direction of the bathroom, "You know."

*The bathroom faker.*

"Would it kill ya to wait a minute? It's your turn."

"I'll be right back."

*Bamboozled. A real Harry Houdini of the smooth getaway.*

And a little personal grooming never hurt anyone either. After dinnertime, I snuggled by my husband's side on the couch. That's when I noticed a wiry gray hair poking out of the center of his left eyebrow. Like a thief, I tried to yank it out, but missed. After a few more tries, he begged me to stop.

"Would it kill ya to pluck that crazy eyebrow?" I said with a laugh. "It's blocking your eye." *Maybe I can tug it out in the middle of the night with tweezers?*

"Don't touch," he said, leaning away. "Trying to watch ESPN here."

"Please. It's so distracting."

"Leave it."

Finding it hard to focus on our conversation, I slipped out of the room to read *I Was a Really Good Mom Before I Had Kids*. In the den, my offspring stared at their respective computer and Xbox in high-tech trances. Unfolded laundry surrounded them like snowdrifts, piled high on every surface. I watched in awe as my daughter shoved the mass to the ground and plunked down her textbooks and backpack. My son took a novel approach and used the laundered clothes as a reclining chair.

*Arrrrg!*

"Would it kill ya to fold the laundry instead of pushing it around?" I asked with a weary shake of my head.

"We're tired," they replied in unison.

Exasperated, I rejoined my husband in the living room. But that rogue hair, which was as long as a pipe cleaner, still fascinated me.

"What?" I said. I was so mesmerized by the hair that I didn't realize he was talking to me.

"Do you want to go out to dinner tomorrow?" he said, apparently for a second time.

"Huh? I can't take my eyes off that hair. Pull it."

"Would it kill ya to stop saying that?" my husband said. He jumped off the couch and tried to hotfoot it out of the room. Not fast enough, I grabbed my man by the arm and held him in a warm embrace.

"I love you," I said, batting my eyes. Then with my thumb and forefinger, I quickly yanked that wild hair right out.

Score one for Mom.

Stacey

# Life is a Beach

by
Ernie Witham

I panicked when I realized that it was Labor Day. For one thing, being self-employed, I had to decide whether to give myself the day off or not. Then I had to call the Hallmark store to find out if they had a card for the occasion. But the biggest problem was my tan, or lack thereof. How the heck did it get to be Labor Day so soon?

I consulted my wife. She, too, was stunned. Not that it was Labor Day, or that, yes indeed, Hallmark did have one card of a rust-colored sun setting on a meat packing plant, but that I was counting myself among that great majority known as "laborer."

"Isn't there some kind of minimum income to qualify?" she wanted to know.

"Writers are exempt," I assured her. Then I suggested that the whole family spend the day at East Beach, near our home in Santa Barbara, California.

"We're going to need a few supplies," she said.

It was busy at the mall. There were end-of-season sales, beginning-of-season sales and offseason sales. One store even had two young women in Santa bikinis holding a sign proclaiming only 113 shopping days until Christmas.

"They have nice tans," my teenage son noted. "Maybe we should ask where they shop."

I thought he had a valid point, but my wife just looked at me and said, "We'll get an umbrella. You get some lotion."

I scanned the mall map for a natural-products store. Being a 21st century man, I'm totally in tune with the use of natural products designed to save the environment, increase our life spans and create millions of dollars in profits for companies that no longer have to use expensive additives, colorings or scents.

The sales clerk at Herbs Are Us glanced up from his copy of *Surf Goddess Monthly,* gave me the once-over and said, "The He-Man Citrus Flip machine is broken." He turned the page and continued reading.

"We're going to the beach," I told him. "I'm devoting the entire day to getting fit and tan."

He looked up again and stared at my white legs for a minute. "Dude, is this like one of those shopper tests or something? Are you from the corporate office? Because I was working my butt off just before you came in, man."

Before I could set him straight, he ambled toward the back of the store, returning 15 minutes later with half a dozen biodegradable plastic bottles.

"Check it out, dude. Here's the pour-opening, pre-sun lotion to prepare your skin, our #8 homogenized dark tanning stain, which you should put on like every five minutes or so, #50 sun block for all that upper forehead thing you've got going on, a large Nosekote, large Earkote and an after-sun aloe product designed to revitalize any skin you ruin. So, do I pass or what?"

"That depends. How much is all that going to cost me?"

"No charge for corporate-office dudes."

"You pass," I told him and with product in hand, left to find my wife. She was at the shoe store helping my daughter try on sandals.

"How long is this going to take?" I asked her.

"I'm not sure," she said. "We've got it narrowed down to either the teal slip-ons or the burgundy lace-ups."

"Where are the boys?"

"Buying a volleyball net and new oars for the rubber raft."

"We're only going for the day."

"I know," she said. "So just buy a cooler big enough for 24 sodas and something for us to drink. Oh, and we'll need stuff to make sandwiches. I made you a list."

I perused both sides of the 8-1/2" x 11" paper, sighed and headed for the deli.

"Throwing a party?" the deli manager wanted to know.

"Nope. Just going to the beach for Labor Day."

"Ahh. That explains the pickled artichoke hearts."

When I finished with the shopping, I returned to my family. I barely recognized our three children—only their freshly capped heads showed above the mound of partially inflated beach paraphernalia.

"Where's your mother?" I asked.

"One of the beach chairs had the wrong pattern," a male voice explained from inside an inner tube. "She said to meet her at the car. When do we eat?"

It took a while to arrange seating, and the mall policeman threatened to give us a ticket if we didn't stop making that squeaking sound of bare flesh on sticky plastic. But finally, after paying $11 for parking, we were on our way to East Beach. Let the tanning begin!

It was my daughter who first noticed. She's always been the observant one. "There's no sun," she said. "I knew I should have gone with the teal."

I stopped the van and watched as a large wisp of fog danced across the empty beach parking lot. Then another and another. I looked at my wife. She was putting on a sweater.

"Oh well," she said. "At least we'll be ready for next year."

I closed the van window and started the heater. I wondered to myself if #8 homogenized dark tanning stain worked with computer screens.

# It's Genetic

by
Lynn Obermoeller

Once a year, my two adult sisters, my brother and I don brightly colored matching T-shirts for our traditional "Sibling Day" outing. No spouses, no children. It's just the four of us acting like crazy kids again—kids whose mom dressed them alike.

Our adventures as a family can be just that—adventurous. We've traveled together by car and train. We've shivered down a river on a raft until our lips were blue and our teeth chattered. And we've laughed ourselves silly during every single outing.

For one such Sibling Day get-together, my husband offered to let me drive his silver Lexus since it provided more room and luxury for our long trip. I was grateful to have the chance to take his extravagant car, but driving it made me nervous—my husband is very particular and very protective about the vehicle. I was warned no messes, no spills, no accidents, *no nothing!* I just knew he would kill me, and my siblings, if we did anything to harm or ruin the Lexus.

Midway through our trip, we pulled into a Kwik Stop to get a snack and use the restroom. I must divulge that the four of us possess the same family trait—we're all a little ditzy. You'd think four heads would be better than one, but in our case, it was just the opposite. None of us can make a decision, and in the case of our quick stop at Kwik Stop, we had a direct run-in with our shared DNA.

In the time it took us to decide which snack to select, we could have cooked a seven-course meal. We followed one another around the store, unsure as to what to buy. My brother finally asked us, "Well, are you going to get something?"

We all shrugged.

My sister answered him: "I will if you do."

She then made the first selection—she grabbed a bag of chips. Her action triggered the rest of us, and we instantly made our selections and went to the register. With drinks and snacks in hand, we trailed one another out the door like a herd of bleating goats, discussing our purchases.

Hitting the key button to unlock the car's doors, I barked orders, "Don't spill one crumb or one drop of anything in this car. You hear me?"

My brother slid into the front seat beside me and sniffed. "Which one of you sprayed yourself with old-lady perfume?" he asked.

I knew it wasn't me reeking. I looked to the back seat. Both my sisters shrugged. No one confessed.

"I'll roll down the windows, blow out the stink," I said as I situated myself into the driver's seat.

Gently placing my coffee cup into the console's drink holder, I was in for a surprise. A quarter inch of the liquid was in the cup holder. "Geezus! How'd this get in here?!" I knew my husband would have a fit if he saw what I saw at that very moment. As I fumbled for a tissue in my purse to sop up the mess, one of my sisters mumbled that her seat felt weird.

Suddenly, in one united "aha!" moment, we ditzy sibs realized our error. But no one spoke. We were in shock. Regaining my wits, I yelled, "Oh, crap! This isn't our car!"

Simultaneously, we reached for the door handles, hollering and snorting, as we jumped out. We couldn't get out of that car fast enough!

We stood in the parking lot and laughed so hard our eyes narrowed to slits and tears ran down our cheeks. Our mouths were open, but only tiny squeaky noises escaped. Once I caught my breath, I realized we needed to make our escape before the real owner of the car appeared. I pointed to my husband's silver Lexus and we ran for our lives.

Continuing on to our destination, we chuckled and poked fun at ourselves. How could we all have nonchalantly—and unknowingly—climbed into a total stranger's car, just because it was silver?

These days, no matter how old we get and despite our matching T-shirts, the genetic link is apparent. Every Sibling Day starts with the same comments, from what we should do to where we should eat. No one cares, and it takes forever for one of us to make the first decision. But we are all in agreement about one thing—whoever is driving can't park next to a same color car!

The siblings, youngest (#4) to oldest (#1):
#4 Ruth, #3 Lynn, #2 Warren and #1 Sue

# Young and Foolish

by
## Sallie Rodman

"Everything packed in the car?" my husband, Frank, asked.

"Everything, including the first aid kit," I replied.

The kids were already sitting in the backseat, itching to get started for their cousins' house. Peter, age seven, sat on one side and sister Karen, age six, sat on the other with Martha, age two, in the middle.

*Lordy, another Fourth of July at the Fitzgeralds,* I thought. I said a silent prayer we would all return home in one piece. You never knew what would happen with this gang of relatives.

Why the tradition started, I haven't a clue . . . probably because my husband's sister Jane and her husband, Bob, had eight kids, a 20-room house and an Olympic-sized swimming pool. It was a no-brainer for them to host the annual event. Kids always outnumbered the adults on the Fourth, and if they ever decided to rebel, we adults would have to run for our lives.

Frank eased the car onto the palm-tree-lined circular driveway. As we pulled up to the house, Uncle Bob stood in the driveway with a beer in his hand to greet. His wild Hawaiian shirt barely covered his Santa belly and from the look on his face, it was obvious he was already feeling no pain.

My husband came to a stop behind a long line of cars— he couldn't wait to get out and join the party. I, on the other hand, dreaded this day and exited slowly.

"Glad ya could make it, glad y'all are here!" Uncle Bob yelled over the rock music blaring from the pool area.

"Oh, it wouldn't be the Fourth without the Fitzgeralds!" my husband yelled back.

We went inside to put our food contribution in the refrigerator. The kids headed straight for the pool, but not before I grabbed them by their arms.

"Whoa, there. You older kids be careful. And Maria, I need to be there to watch you, sweetie. You're too young to go in the pool alone. Wait for me."

With the beer stashed, I slipped into my suit, threw on a sarong and took Maria by the hand. It wasn't hard to find the pool. You just had to follow the blasting rock-and-roll music to the sea of bobbing heads. I looked for my other kids and after a brief moment of panic, found them swimming and having fun. A couple of dogs ran around the pool area, yipping excitedly at the kids in the pool.

I put Maria in the pool's shallow end, on the steps, and settled down in a deck chair. The other mothers said hello, but it was hard to chat when you could only see their lips move.

After a half-hour sitting in the 90-degree heat, I decided

to go in the house for a cola. I really wanted a beer, but I knew one of us had to stay sober and it wasn't going to be Frank. Spotting him talking to Uncle Bob, I ran over.

"Hey, babe—can you please watch Maria? I want to get a cola and don't want to drag her out of the pool."

"Sure thing, no problem. I'll keep an eye on her," he said, heading down to the pool.

In the house, the kitchen was mobbed with people—kids grabbing colas, guys hunkered down by the kegs and women trying to keep the kids from snacking away all the chips and dips.

As I stuck my head in the refrigerator, I saw another head beside me. I pulled up so fast I knocked myself silly on the top shelf.

"Frank, what are you doing here? I thought you were watching Maria!"

"Oh, she's fine. I asked one of the kids to watch her."

"You what?!"

"Well, there's enough of them out there," he replied with no shame whatsoever. I shot out the door and down to the pool. Luckily, one of the aunts had seen Maria alone and went over to watch her.

"Sorry!" I yelled apologetically, motioning to Maria.

"No problem," she mouthed, hands upturned.

Soon it was late afternoon and time for the barbecue. Eight grills were set up on the huge patio.

Cooking for 72 people was no mean feat. A few times, a hot dog rolled off the grill and one of the dogs would run off with it.

Finally, kids sated and adults relaxed from a keg or two, it was dark and time for the fireworks. The adults lined up their deck chairs and the kids scrambled for seats on the edge of the patio.

"Got the hose ready?!" Uncle Bob yelled.

"Sure thing," his oldest boy, Carl, called back. "Ready when you are!"

Soon the fireworks show started and it lasted for nearly an hour since everyone brought some goodies to share. When we got down to the last firework—a Double Blaster—Uncle Bob got up on the patio wall and asked for quiet.

"I have a big treat for y'all. You may think that the fireworks are almost finished, but I'm proud to say that this year, my sons have been down in our basement cooking up their own batch of fireworks."

A groan went up from the mothers in the crowd. Homemade fireworks! This would not turn out good.

Uncle Bob and Aunt Jane had eight boys, all a year apart in age. They were a handful, and sometimes I thought that with Uncle Bob, Jane felt as if she had nine boys. And this was one of those times. "Leave it to Bob to let the boys make fireworks," Jane said, shaking her head.

Suddenly there was a big *BANG!*

Everyone looked over to the side where the Fitzgerald boys were gathered. The boom had originated there and sparks were flying around J.J.'s feet.

"My fireworks! My fireworks!" yelled the youngest Fitzgerald boy, J.J. A brown paper bag holding his precious few fireworks was smoldering on the lawn.

"I lost all my fireworks," J.J. blubbered through his tears.

"Serves you right," his older brother Carl yelled. "Told you not to keep lighting those matches."

"Oh, stop crying like a baby," his next eldest brother said.

The chaos went on until J.J. finally settled down on the patio concrete to sulk and watch his brothers set off their own creations.

After they finished, Uncle Bob went into the grand finale and set off a bottle rocket. It failed to launch and landed instead on the neighbor's garage roof.

"Hose!" he yelled to one of the boys, motioning toward the flames eating away at the shingles.

Everyone watched in awe as Uncle Bob stood atop the fence to put out the fire. During all the commotion and possible house fire, Jane came around and handed out watermelon. She seemed unfazed.

By then, it was 11 o'clock and everyone was dragging. Tired and weary, kids and parents headed to their cars. Before we were out of the driveway, Karen, Maria and Peter were fast asleep in the backseat.

I thanked God all the way home that we had survived another Fourth at the Fitzgeralds'.

Our kids and cousins are all grown now, some with children of their own. At a recent family reunion, we reminisced about those bygone Fourths.

"Wasn't that the best fun ever?" Maria asked.

"Oh, yeah!" her cousins chimed in.

"I hated them," said Aunt Jane.

"You did?" I asked. "Gosh I'm glad to hear you say that. I did too."

"So did I," said the other aunts, in unison.

"Why did we do it if we hated them so much?" I asked.

"Because we were young and foolish, and so years later, like today, we could look back at those family gatherings and laugh," Jane replied.

And she's right. It makes my therapist laugh, too, every time I tell him the story.

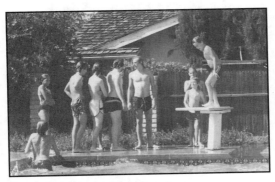

Fourth of July at the Fitzgeralds'

# Laura Ingalls Wilder Totally Lied

by

Tracy Winslow

I always loved kids and couldn't wait to have a family of my own. As a child, I coveted everyone's baby. I watched everyone's children whenever asked. I was even a camp counselor. My best friend's daughter called me "Mum-ma." My destiny to be the perfect mother with the perfect family was written in the stars!

I knew exactly what it was going to be like to have the most wonderful life and family. After my family all happily pitched in and cleaned up the kitchen after dinner, which, I might add, was a meal made mostly from fresh vegetables from our garden, we'd sit around the fireplace and talk about our hopes, dreams and the latest *NY Times* bestseller. Husband would then read the *Wall Street Journal* and Kid #1, *Harry Potter*. Kid #2 would play with our kittens on my spotless floors and

I, wearing size-4 jeans, would knit my latest beautiful sweater while sitting on our gorgeous davenport. And there would even be singing. Not by me, of course.

My family would be a hybrid of Laura Ingalls Wilder's *Little House on the Prairie*, as well as *The Secret Garden* and *Anne of Green Gables,* with just the right splash of *Ramona*. My children would be like the altruistic March girls in Louisa May Alcott's *Little Women*. I've read tens of thousands of books, which clearly makes me an expert on parenting. I just needed to fill in the "husband" blank and get this party started!

Fast forward a few years. I had a family. Husband, check. Kid #1: five-year-old Lena, check. Kid #2: two-year-old Emmeline, check. Perhaps if I had read *Sybil* or *The Exorcist,* I would have been a little more prepared for what I was about to face.

Here's a snippet of family life in the Winslow household yesterday:

"Lena, for the love of God, brush your teeth. The sea monkeys have left their tank and taken up residency in your mouth."

"No, Emmeline, you cannot feed the goldfish again. They will explode—again."

"Lena, seriously, brush your teeth."

"Mommy, it's SOOOO not fair that you won't let me have anything I want for breakfast! I'm probably going to starve to death and die and it's all your fault because you won't let me eat cheese popcorn or Pez for breakfast."

"Moooooommmmyyyy! Emmeline won't share your phone!"

The small scuffle in the living room led to tears. They ran

into the kitchen. Emmeline held out my iPhone.

"Lena, did you put a sticker on the front of my phone?!"

"Well, she wouldn't share it. So if I can't watch the phone, no one can," said Lena-in-charge.

I try consequences. "OK. You may not use the phone until after school because you decided to put a sticker on the screen, which you know is wrong."

"Well, that's it, Emmeline. I no longer am your sister. We are done. Forever. Until the end of time. So don't even ask to play with me. Ever. Again."

"OK, well, now that you have all this free time on your hands, how about you go brush your teeth?" I coaxed.

I look at the table. "Emmeline, where's the waffle I just toasted for you?" I hear a flush. *Oh, dear . . . thank God we rent,* I thought.

"Lena, please, do not make me yell. I am losing my patience. Go brush your teeth. We have to go to school in a few minutes."

"No. I do not need to brush my teeth because I have decided that I am no longer a member of this family. Did you not read the memo?"

I cursed in Spanish under my breath. And all of this happened before 8 A.M.

Later that day, I broke up fist fights over My Little Ponies and who got to flush the potty in the dollhouse. I cleaned the entire box of raisins off the floor after Emmeline made it "rain." Two seconds later, it looked as if the American Girl doll store had thrown up in my living room. I picked up toys, sippy cups and children that had fallen off some ladder-like object used to climb up to the fish tank because Emmeline wanted to tickle the fish. And Lena required rescuing as she had been closed into the couch's ottoman by Emmeline, because wolves live in dens.

By the time dinner rolled around, I was ready to feed my girls whatever fell out of the pantry first—or crawled out of the vegetable drawer. I mean, mold is green, right? I poured a bunch of quinoa in a pot and added something that resembled protein, happy that I had managed to pull something together before Husband arrived home. Once he did, his only comment about the meal was, "Oh, great. Whale sperm for dinner."

What about my fantasy of cleaning up dinner dishes as a family? No way! Lena pulled out yet another number from the soundtrack of *Cinderella Strikes Back: The Bitter Years* and she and her sister sang their own version, "I do not clean. No, no. You are not the boss of me!" Backup singer Emmeline chimed in, "No clean. No, no. I the boss."

I was so tired I began to contemplate curling up in a ball under the couch, resting my head on the dust bunnies and rocking myself to sleep. But I knew they'd find me there. They always find me. And they'd probably want food and wouldn't settle for petrified french fries within arm's reach.

I know what my epitaph will read: *She just lay around all day reading silly books about the life she wished she had.*

Sigh . . . someone owes me a refund. Yeah, I'm looking at you, Laura Ingalls Wilder.

# Family Police Blotter: June Edition

by
Timothy Martin

It's been a busy month for Mom and Dad Martin when it comes to keeping their family in check:

*June 1* (Advice to Resident) Martin parents received report from high school teacher that teenager was not turning in homework on time. Matter was discussed with son who lives in bedroom, plays video games nonstop and insists on remaining isolated. Response was the usual eye rolling, one-syllable grunts and a half-hearted agreement to knuckle down and try harder. No action taken.

*June 3* (Mental Abuse) After reading about the importance of spending family time together, Mom turns it into a daily requirement. Whether enduring an awkward dinner at home, sitting unpleasantly at a boring school event or staring blankly at The Family Channel on TV, our little clan makes an immense effort to spend plenty of uncomfortable, silent quality time together. As far as anyone knows, we are a normal family. Case closed.

*June 4* (Shopping Infraction) Credit card confiscated from 16-year-old daughter whose life revolves around malls and sparkling vampires. When queried about excessive use of card, daughter had a diva-level meltdown and asked if she was being *Punk'd.* Mom drove a spike of logic through the opaque mist of vapor that floats through her teenage head by explaining that distressed jeans and designer purses were not considered necessities. Daughter departed in haste.

*June 6* (Sleeping Violation) Kids sleeping in on weekends. Way in. Often until 5 P.M. Mom explained that teens have growing bodies, their brains are going through loads of changes and their sleep patterns are off. They need loads of daily rest, especially when they stay up all night watching movies and playing online video games. Dad suggested that a better name for teenagers might be "vampires" or "creatures of the night."

*June 9* (Conflict of Interest) Meeting called regarding after-school snacks. Mom voted for roasted chickpeas, sunflower seeds, blue corn sea-salted chips and air-popped organic popcorn. Other family members noted that such healthy items made the term "snack" lose all meaning and instead suggested Doritos, Snickers, soda pop, Big Macs and various bacon-wrapped, deep-fried *Fear Factor* food-like items. No compromise found.

*June 12* (Electronics Abuse) Daily TV, computer, iPod, iPhone and Xbox use by minors found to be far exceeding posted time limits. Dad given a blanket order to round up and confiscate all electronic doo-dads, gee-gaws and gizmos and place them under lock and key. Despite numerous and loud complaints, Martin household was officially placed off the grid for one full week.

*June 16* (Noise Ordinance Offense) Mom and Dad noted that teenage son was playing music at cranial imploding, ears-fell-off-and-landed-on-the-floor volume. Son accused parents of living in a self-imposed Dark Age. Verbal conflict ensued. Teenager was informed about the penalties for insubordination and music was immediately turned down. Teen's erratic behavior attributed to hip-hop music.

*June 19* (Makeup Misdemeanor) Teary-eyed daughter who craves independence beyond the war-torn lands of family authoritarianism said that she hates her life—big time. Her problem stems from an inability to cope with a home environment that "totally sucks," a "complete lack of privacy" and not being allowed to wear makeup to a school basketball game. Daughter also repeatedly stated that life will be unbearable until she turns 18 and moves out. Parents in complete agreement.

*June 21* (Highway Faux Pas) Mom in a panic when car breaks down on busy highway. Additionally, her cellular telephone quit working. Upon Dad's arrival, it was discovered that 1) phone needed a charge, and 2) car was just out of gas. Problems were quickly resolved and blame was placed squarely on husband's shoulders. No action taken.

*June 25* (Decency Encroachment) Teenage son found

wearing baggy pants, unlaced shoes and backward-facing ball cap. Parents demanded that he hitch up his pants, tie his shoes and turn his cap around before leaving home. After moaning and complaining about house rules, homeboy reluctantly complied with requests. But not before stating that parents suck joy from life like the dusk swallows daylight. Teenager left in a huff.

*June 27* (Theft Investigation) Dad alleged that he was robbed of his wallet by unknown parties between 0800 and 1700 hours. ID, credit cards and cash reported missing. Police called. Search party formed. Minutes later, it was ascertained that wallet had been left on bedroom dresser that morning. Complainant slapped himself upside the head for being such a numbskull. No further action required.

*June 29* (Illegal Loitering) When asked what he was doing all day, teenager stated that he'd been hanging out with friends. Dad immediately put him to work mowing lawn and trimming hedges. Son expressed dismay and was told by Dad that hanging out may seem harmless enough, but it distracts kids from more important goals like putting your nose to the grindstone"and holding your feet to the fire and giving it your all. Hanging out is a form of loitering that often leads to far worse things, such as easin' or chillin'. Today it's hanging out. Tomorrow it might be stokin', smokin' or tokin'. That's the problem, explained Dad. You never know where it's going take you.

*June 31* (Code Booze) Bottle of wine uncorked by parents. Family life goes on as usual. No further actions are contemplated.

# NYMB Series Founders

Together, Dahlynn and Ken McKowen have 60-plus years of professional writing, editing, publication, marketing and public relations experience. Full-time authors and travel writers, the two have such a large body of freelance work that when they reached more than 2,000 articles, stories and photographs published, they stopped counting. And the McKowens are well-respected ghostwriters, having worked with CEOs and founders of some of the nation's biggest companies. They have even ghostwritten for a former U.S. president and a few California governors and elected officials.

From 1999 to 2009, Ken and Dahlynn were consultants and coauthors for *Chicken Soup for the Soul*, where they collaborated with series founders Jack Canfield and Mark Victor Hansen on several books such as *Chicken Soup for the Entrepreneur's Soul; Chicken Soup for the Soul in Menopause; Chicken Soup for the Fisherman's Soul;* and *Chicken Soup for the Soul: Celebrating Brothers and Sisters*. They also edited and ghost-created many more Chicken titles during their tenure, with Dahlynn reading more than 100,000 story submissions.

For highly acclaimed outdoor publisher Wilderness Press, the McKowens' books include *Best of Oregon and Washington's Mansions, Museums and More; The Wine-Oh! Guide to California's Sierra Foothills* and national award-winning *Best of California's Missions, Mansions and Museums.*

Under the Publishing Syndicate banner, the couple authored and published *Wine Wherever: In California's Mid-Coast & Inland Region*, and are actively researching wineries for *Wine Wherever: In California's Paso Robles Region*, the second book in the Wine Wherever series.

Ken with Dahlynn and Dahlynn's kids Lahre and Shawn, during a trip to Disneyland (that's Tinker Bell they're holding in their hands), 2004

Ken with his grandson Jake, adult son Jason and stepson Shawn (front), 2009

## About Linda O'Connell

Linda O'Connell is a multi-published writer, early-childhood teacher, writing instructor, mentor and founding member of her outstanding critique group—Wild Women Wielding Pens. Her stories of hope, inspiration and humor have been published in several *Not Your Mother's Books*, 22 *Chicken Soup for the Soul* books, *Sasee Magazine* and many other national publications.

Early family life colored Linda's writing in many ways. Her free-spirited parents didn't put down roots in one place for very long. She and her younger brother were always the new kids on the block and in school. Her life stories have paid off in the form of many publishing credits. She blogs at http://lindaoconnell.blogspot.com.

Linda's budding writing career began at age 10 when she won a large piece of yellow "teacher's chalk" as a Bingo prize. She used the side of her dad's faded green car as a chalkboard. Linda didn't just teach a lesson that day—she learned one. She's been learning ever since. In her 38th year as a very creative prekindergarten teacher, Linda continues not only to teach classes, but she still enjoys taking classes.

Linda and her husband, Bill, live in St. Louis, Missouri. They have a blended family of four adult children. Nine grandchildren—ages six through 24—call her "Nana." They have given her many laugh lines. Every family gathering results in hilarity and enough writing material for another personal essay.

Linda keeps journals for each grandchild and presents them to the children on their 18th birthdays. Rubbing a grandchild's back, snuggling with the youngest, listening to the older ones as they confide their dreams and wishes, cheering them on as they play sports, watching them grow way too fast—these are the things that make her family life fulfilling.

Linda and husband Bill (above left), with her adult kids Jason and Tracey (above right) and with youngest granddaughter Nicole (right)

# Contributor Bios

**Diana M. Amadeo** is an award-winning author from the Greater Boston area. She enjoys family time with her husband, adult children and grandchildren. Her wooded sanctuary comes alive when the zip line, trampoline and fire pit are in use. When everyone goes home, Diana becomes a recluse in the greenhouse.

**Jerry W. Baker,** a native Texan, resides with wife Kathy and three fur kids: Hank, Samantha and Abby. His alma mater is Texas Tech University. After college, Jerry proudly served in the U.S. Marine Corps before starting a lifelong career in the life-insurance industry. He has contributed to three NYMB books.

**Jenny Beatrice** lives in St. Louis with her husband, three kids, mother, dog and bunny. Her sense of humor, passion for writing and career in communications helps her spin her family's memories and mishaps into stories that make you smile. Jenny blogs at correctionsandclarifications.com.

**Sylvia Bright-Green,** in her 35-year writing career, has been published in 15 anthologies and co-authored two books. She has published hundreds of manuscripts in newspapers, magazines and in local and national publications. She is now awaiting word of when her books on humor, spirituality and sex will be published.

**Debra Ayers Brown** is a creative nonfiction writer, blogger, magazine humor columnist and award-winning marketing professional. Enjoy her stories in multiple editions of *NYMB, Chicken Soup for the Soul, Guideposts, Woman's World* and more. She graduated from UGA and earned her MBA from The Citadel. Connect with her at www.About.Me/DebraAyersBrown.

**Sallie Wagner Brown** writes stories inspired by her kids who think they are grown up, her dogs who think they are her kids and the rest of her crazy, step-half family. She retired from teaching English at age 50 and bought a used red Corvette. She knows she isn't grown up.

**Christine Cacciatore** is married to a wonderful man, has three great kids, a new granddaughter, and one ridiculous dog. She and her sister Jennifer Starkman co-wrote and recently published *Baylyn, Bewitched*, first in *The Whitfield Witch Series*, available as an ebook on Amazon, Barnes & Noble and Smashwords.

**Kathe Campbell** lives her dream on a Montana mountain with her mammoth donkeys, a Keeshond and a few kitties. Three children, 11 grandchildren and four greats round out the herd. She is a prolific writer on Alzheimer's and a contributing author to *Chicken Soup for the Soul*, medical journals and magazines.

**Barbara Carpenter,** award-winning poet and storyteller, resides in Southern Illinois. As well as the *Starlight, Starbright* family saga trilogy, she has written memoirs for two professional men and is currently writing another. A regular contributor to the *NYMB* and *Chicken Soup* anthologies, she also enjoys painting and quilting.

**Liane Kupferberg Carter** is a journalist whose articles and essays have appeared in many publications, including *The New York Times*, the *Chicago Tribune* and *The Huffington Post*. She writes a monthly column for *Autism After 16* and is currently completing a memoir. You can follow her at http://www.huffingtonpost.com/liane-kupferberg-carter.

**Lisa Ricard Claro** is an award-winning short-story author and Pushcart Prize nominee. She resides in Georgia with her husband, two dogs and three cats, and dreams of living at the beach. Lisa loves to hear from readers. Please email her at lisa.r.claro@gmail.com and visit her blog www.lisaricardclaro.com.

**Shari Courter** married her high-school sweetheart Ron in 1993. They have one son, Zac, and three daughters—Aubrey, Kearstin and Caymen. Shari is a stay-at-home mom, a licensed massage therapist and a Zumba instructor. In her spare time, she enjoys blogging about her family's antics at CloseCourters.Blogspot.com.

**Mona Dawson** lives in Northern California, loves her family, cool weather, Pacific Grove and anything chocolate. She mostly writes for herself and family, but with much encouragement, has now decided to share her stories with everyone else. You may contact "MonaD" at closedmouth0@yahoo.com.

**Terri Duncan,** a high school administrator, is a devoted wife and mother of two grown children. She hopes they support her in her retirement so she can pursue her dream of writing. She has authored numerous short stories and published *Camping Reservations: Body of Lies*, a book for young readers.

**Norine Dworkin-McDaniel** created the illustrated humor blog "Science of Parenthood" and serves as its Chief of Scientific Snarkiness. When she's not blogging about the mysteries of parenting a seven-year-old, she works as a freelance writer. Her articles have appeared in *More, Health, Parents, American Baby* and *Redbook*.

**Laura Edwards-Ray** lives in St. Louis' suburbs with her husband Tom and two daughters. She's tirelessly trying to perfect being a mother, wife, law firm representative, cook, speaker and author—failing miserably on all ends. She is the author of a four-volume series, *Brain Dead in the Burbs* (2010–2015).

**Terri Elders** lives near Colville, Washington with two dogs and three cats. A lifelong writer and editor, her stories have appeared in dozens of periodicals and anthologies. She's a co-creator for *Not Your Mother's Book...On Travel* and the upcoming *On Sharing Secrets* and *My First Time*. She blogs at atouchoftarragon.blogspot.com.

**Lawrence D. Elliott** is an author, *Chicken Soup for the Soul* and *The Huffington Post* contributor and has been a guest on the popular radio show "The Daily Wrap from *The Wall Street Journal* with Michael Castner." Born in San Diego, California, he currently lives in Bensheim, Germany.
Visit him at http://www.lawrenceelliott.com.

**Melissa Face** lives in southeastern Virginia and enjoys traveling to New England with her family. She teaches high school English and writes when she is not grading student work. Melissa's essays have been published in numerous magazines and anthologies. Email Melissa at writermsface@yahoo.com.

**Melissa Fuoss** is an alternative-education teacher, mother of two adorable boys and a wife to a man who knew he would marry her the day he met her. She was raised in St. Louis by a dad who inspired her with his love of life and a mom who was never afraid to keep it real.

**Paprika Furstenburg** was born with poor coordination and a penchant for giggling. This combination has taught her to find humor in unexpected places. Paprika shares her central New Jersey home with three creatures that always make her laugh: her husband and two cats. She blogs at www.goodhumored.wordpress.com.

**Bud Gardner,** former writing instructor at American River College, was named the "Most Inspirational Writing Coach in America." His students earned more than $10,000,000 for writing and selling 10,000 articles and stories and 200 books. He is co-author of *Chicken Soup for the Writer's Soul,* a *New York Times* bestseller.

**T'Mara Goodsell** is an award-winning, multi-genre writer and teacher who lives near St. Louis, Missouri. She has written for various anthologies, newspapers and publications and is currently working on a book for young adults. The names in her story have been changed to protect the guilty.

**Susan Guerrero** has been writing professionally for several decades. She has a journalism degree from the University of Arizona in Tucson and has written for newspapers for many years. She has also written more than 1,400 posts for her online blog titled "Writing Straight from the Heart."

**Stacey Gustafson** has a humor column, "Are You Kidding Me?" Her stories are published in *Chicken Soup for the Soul* and *Not Your Mother's Book...On Being a Woman, Travel, Parent* and *Home Improvement.* Her work appears in *Generation Fabulous* and *ZestNow.* Follow her at staceygustafson.com and on Twitter @mepaint.

**Cathy C. Hall** is a writer from the sunny South. Her essays, short stories, poetry and articles have been published in markets for both children and adults. She also blogs about all things writerly. Come read what she's been up to at www.c-c-hall.com.

**Nancy Hershorin** grew up in Fresno, California, where she raised three daughters. She has traveled extensively and lived for several years in Western Australia. Nancy loves to cook and enjoys writing amusing stories about her life. Now retired, she lives in Eugene, Oregon to be close to her four-year-old granddaughter.

**Mary-Lane Kamberg** is a professional writer in Olathe, Kansas. She is the author of *The "I Don't Know How To Cook" Book* and, with Rolland Love, the cookbook *Homegrown in the Ozarks.* She is co-leader of the Kansas City Writers Group.

**Janet Sheppard Kelleher** is honored to have won a 2013 Carrie McCray Literary Award for nonfiction. A newspaper columnist, Janet is creating a collection of Southern stories called *Havin' My Cotton-Pickin' Say.* Her humorous memoir, *Big C, Little Ta-Tas*—about kicking breast cancer's butt—debuts in 2014.

**Paul Kent** might have been president of the AMA (Average Men of America) if he weren't so darned average. The husband of one, father of three and author of several—including *Playing with Purpose: Baseball Devotions*—he enjoys reading history and watching trains. Mushrooms are definitely *not* among his favorite things.

**Jamie Krakover** is an aerospace engineer by day and a writer by night. She loves books, movies, dancing, Twitter and spending time with her family. Jamie lives in St. Louis, Missouri with her Cavachon, Sophie. She blogs at http://jamiekrakover. blogspot.com.

**Margaret Lalich** is a writer, speech-language pathologist and education specialist from Northern California. She's a believer and a relentless optimist who loves great music, good food and hearty humor. She seeks out the laughter and writes of the loves, tears and joys of discovery she finds in everyday life.

**Cathi LaMarche,** a composition teacher, novelist, essayist and writing coach, spends most of her days immersed in the written word. Her stories appear in over 20 anthologies. She resides in Missouri with her husband, two children and three spoiled dogs. Cathi is currently working on her second novel.

**Lisa McManus Lange** still battles the never-ending fight against technology—says she who writes on a laptop. Find her slice of life stories in other *Not Your Mother's Books*, as well as *Chicken Soup for the Soul*. Contact her at www.lisamcmanuslange.blogspot.com or at lisamc2010@yahoo.ca.

**Morton A. Levy, M.D.**, a hematologist-oncologist whose poetry and memoirs have been published in literary magazines and anthologies, is now enjoying a second career in his retirement—memoir writing. A prevailing theme in this work is documenting growing up and coming of age in the 1940s and 1950s.

**David Martin's** humor and political satire have appeared in many publications including *The New York Times*, the *Chicago Tribune* and *Smithsonian Magazine*. His latest humor collection *Screams & Whispers* is available on Amazon.com. David lives in Ottawa, Canada with his wife Cheryl and their daughter Sarah.

**Glady Martin** loves to write. Writing has led her through the trials of life, death, heartbreak and happiness. Wanting to laugh lots more in this last chapter of her life, Glady is now writing funny, silly and true-life stories as a way to focus on those good memories. Email: gladymartin1@shaw.ca

**Timothy Martin** is a columnist for the *Times-Standard* newspaper and the author of *Rez Rock; There's Nothing Funny About Running; Summer With Dad; Wimps Like Me* and *Why Run If No One Is Chasing You?* Tim is a contributing author to numerous *Chicken Soup* books and two NYMB books.

**Madeline McEwen** writes to maintain sanity in her madcap family life. Bifocaled, flat-footed and middle-aged since birth, Madeline juggles autism and Alzheimer's with as much good cheer as possible on a Wednesday in San Jose in jolly old California.

**Laurel McHargue** was raised as "Daughter #4" of five girls in Braintree, Massachusetts where she lived until heading off to Smith College, followed by the United States Military Academy. Her constant quest for adventure landed her in Leadville, Colorado where she resides with her husband. Read more at www.leadvillelaurel.com.

**Mike McHugh** is author of "The Dang Yankee," a humorous column about life in Louisiana and the world at large. His column appears in *The Louisiana Jam*, a publication covering Southwest Louisiana and Southeast Texas. He also has two stories in *Not Your Mother's Book . . . On Home Improvement.*

**Pat Nelson** is co-creator of Not Your Mother's Book . . . On Being a Parent. She is accepting stories for two additional books she is co-creating: *NYMB . . . On Being a Grandparent* and *On Working for a Living.* Visit her website at www.Storystorm.US.

**Tori Nichols** is a writer-poet. She lives in Southern Illinois with wonderful family members who unwittingly supply material for humorous stories. Her work can also be found in *Chicken Soup for the Nurse's Soul: Second Dose, Not Your Mother's Book . . . On Home Improvement* and *Cynic Magazine.* Message her at www.torinichols.com.

**Sheree K. Nielsen**, a multi-award-winning writer and photographer, pens inspirational essays interweaving travel, nature and family. Publications include *Missouri Life* and *AAA Midwest/Southern Traveler.* She's frequently seen sipping cappuccinos and riding around town with her Doggle-wearing Australian Shepherd, Sabrina. Loves: scuba diving; beachcombing, dark chocolate, hubby and four animal children. www.shereenielsen.wordpress.com

**Lynn Obermoeller** is a published, multi-genre writer from St. Louis, Missouri. Her favorite form of writing is epistolary. Find out more at her website, Lynn's Lost Art of Letter Writing at www.lynnobermoeller.com, or follow her blog Present Letters at http://lynnobermoeller.blogspot.com.

**Frank Ramirez** and his wife Jennie live in the Snake Spring Valley, the reddest part of a blue state (Pennsylvania) where their voting record is the only bone of contention between them and their neighbors. In addition to their three children, they share four grandchildren. Frank is a writer and a pastor.

**Cappy Hall Rearick** is a syndicated newspaper columnist, award-winning short-story writer and author of six published books and five successful columns. Featured by the Erma Bombeck Writers Workshop as a Humor Writer of the Month, Rearick's humor and short fiction have been read and enjoyed in anthologies throughout the country.

**John Reas** discovered his passion for writing rather late in life. This is his sixth story for the *Not Your Mother's Book* series, and he's wondering who would be a good actor to portray his father if "The Toupee" ever made it to the silver screen.

**Kendall Roderick** has a handful of published short stories, but strives to be a full-time writer. When she isn't writing, she is a graphic designer. Kendall enjoys her days at the computer with her furry children and her husband, who reads over her stories every night.

**Sallie Rodman** received her certificate in professional writing from the California State University, Long Beach. Her stories have appeared in NYMB, *Chicken Soup for the Soul, Cup of Comfort* and other magazines and anthologies. She loves writing about true events that touch us, make us laugh or warm our hearts. Email: sa.rodman@verizon.net

**Sioux Roslawski** is Virginia and Ian's mom, Jason's mother-in-law and Riley's "Grammy." During the day she teaches third grade. In her spare time, she freelances and blogs (http://siouxspage.blogspot.com). Sioux is one of the five founding members of the infamous writing critique group—the WWWPs.

**Verna Simms** is a freelance writer. Twelve years ago, she joined the Jefferson County Writers' Society and began recording light-heartened slices of her life. She has been published in numerous magazines and anthologies and writes a column for the local paper—*The Leader.* Verna enjoys reading, swimming and family.

**Bobby Barbara Smith** is a writer and a musician/singer from Bull Shoals, Arkansas. Her humorous, heartfelt short stories have been published in *Not Your Mother's Book . . . On Dogs, Stupid Kid, and Home Improvement,* plus other anthologies and e-zines. Bobby blogs at http://indy113.wordpress.com.

**Jim Tobalski,** after 37 years in management and marketing communications, has uncorked his quirky and humorous outlook by writing just for fun. In his blog www.MrIDo.com, Jim parodies his skills as a husband and relationship master. He also speaks about communication skills at conferences, universities and random hardware stores.

**Lisa Tognola** is a freelance writer who pens the blog Mainstreetmusingsblog. com, which highlights the humorous side of suburban life—the good, the bad and the ugly. She is a parenting and lifestyles contributor at Manilla.com and contributes to online magazine More.com. Twitter @lisatognola

**Pat Wahler** is a grant writer by day and writer of fiction and essays by night. Her work has been published in dozens of local and national venues. A lifelong animal lover, Pat ponders critters, writing and life's little mysteries at www.critteralley.blogspot.com.

**Tracy Winslow** was voted Top 25 Funniest Moms at Circle of Moms/PopSugar and Top 10 Funniest Moms on the web by Parent Society. Besides crafting cocktails with Zoloft, Tracy Winslow can be found crying into her coffee over her stretch marks, Ouija-boarding her deceased metabolism or writing a humor blog: http://www.momaical.com.

**Ernie Witham** writes the nationally syndicated column "Ernie's World" for the *Montecito Journal* in Santa Barbara, California. He is the author of two humor books, leads humor writing workshops and is on the permanent faculty of the Santa Barbara Writer's Conference. His stories have also appeared in three NYMB books.

# Story Permissions

*Spaghetti Squash* © 2012 Diana M. Amadeo
*The High Lonesome* © 2013 Jerry W. Baker
*Food Fighters* © 2013 Jenny R. Beatrice
*The Power of Suggestion* © 1995 Sylvia Bright-Green
*Close, But No Cigar* © 2013 Debra Brown
*Dazed and Confused* © 2010 Sallie Wagner Brown
*I Should Have Listened* © 2012 Christine M. Cacciatore
*The Witches of Yellowstone* © 2010 Kathleen M. Campbell
*Battle Strategies* © 2013 Barbara Carpenter
*36 Ways to Wreck Your Vacation* © 2010 Liane Kupferberg Carter
*A Word Repeated* © 2013 Lisa Ricard Claro
*Take Me Out to the Ballgame* © 2010 Shari Courter
*Head Over Heels* © 2013 Mona E. Dawson
*Nana Got the Last Word* © 2013 Mona E. Dawson
*Payback's a Bitch* © 2006 Terri Duncan
*You Bet Your M&M's!* © 2012 Norine Dworkin-McDaniel
*The Real Facts of Life* © 2010 Laura Edwards-Ray
*Killing Them with Kindness* © 2012 Theresa J. Elders
*Doing It Right* © 2008 Lawrence D. Elliott
*Farmer on the Dell* © 2011 Melissa Seeley Face
*Badass in the Badlands* © 2013 Melissa Ann Fuoss
*Pigs in Blankets* © 2012 Paprika Furstenburg
*When Hummingbirds Call* © 2009 Bud Gardner
*A Certain Air About Her* © 2011 T'Mara Goodsell
*One in a Million* © 2013 Susan Guerrero
*Would It Kill Ya?* © 2012 Stacey Gustafson
*The Bathroom Mystery* © 2013 Cathy C. Hall
*Oh, Daddy!* © 2013 Nancy P. Caldwell Hershorin
*Never Again!* © 2013 Mary-Lane Kamberg
*Telltale Possessions* © 2013 Janet Sheppard Kelleher
*On the Defensive* © 2012 Paul Kent
*Seder Insanity* © 2012 Jamie Krakover
*Blended* © 2013 Margaret Lalich
*Are You Game?* © 2013 Cathi R. LaMarche
*Standing My Ground* © 2013 Lisa Lange
*An Almost Perfect Lady* © 2011 Morton A. Levy

*The Last Camping Trip* © 2006 David Joseph Martin
*What Goes Around Comes Around* © 2014 Glady Martin
*Family Police Blotter: June Edition* © 2012 Timothy Martin
*Nonna's Sage Advice* © 2013 Madeline C. McEwen-Asker
*Home Movies* © 2012 Laurel J. McHargue
*From Soup to Putz* © 2013 John Michael McHugh
*The Grand Pause* © 2013 Dahlynn McKowen
*Foolish Kisses* © 2005 Patricia Nelson
*Bunny Love* © 2013 Victoria L. Nichols
*Mom's Best Advice* © 2013 Sheree K. Nielsen
*It's Genetic* © 2013 Lynn M. Obermoeller
*The Family that Votes Together . . .* © 2012 Frank Ramirez
*Thanksgiving is Relative* © 2010 Kathlyn Hall Rearick
*The Toupee* © 2012 John Reas
*Closing Time* © 2013 Kendall Roderick
*Young and Foolish* © 2012 Sallie A. Rodman
*Leaving My Mark* © 2013 Sioux Roslawski
*When There's a Will . . .* © 2009 Verna L. Simms
*Crazy Old Saint* © 2013 Bobby Smith
*Musky-in-Law* © 2011 James Tobalski
*Getting Our Just Desserts* © 2013 Lisa Tognola
*The Big Announcement* © 2012 Patricia M. Wahler
*Laura Ingalls Wilder Totally Lied* © 2012 Tracy E. Winslow
*Life is a Beach* © 1996 Ernie Witham

# Photo Credits

Except as indicated below, the photos in this book were provided by the story contributors and used with their permission.

Cover photo: Andresr/Shutterstock.com
Page 43: photos provided by the Dayton Dragons
Page 85: photo provided by Amy Phillips

# Publishing Syndicate

Publishing Syndicate LLC is an independent book publisher based in Northern California. The company has been in business for more than a decade, mainly providing writing, ghostwriting and editing services for major publishers. In 2011, Publishing Syndicate took the next step and expanded into a full-service publishing house.

The company is owned by married couple Dahlynn and Ken McKowen. Dahlynn is the CEO and publisher, and Ken serves as president and managing editor.

Publishing Syndicate's mission is to help writers and authors realize personal success in the publishing industry, and, at the same time, provide an entertaining reading experience for its customers. From hands-on book consultation and their very popular and free monthly *Wow Principles* publishing tips e-newsletter to forging book deals with both new and experienced authors and launching three new anthology series, Publishing Syndicate has created a powerful and enriching environment for those who want to share their writing with the world.

**Publishing Syndicate**
PO Box 607
Orangevale CA 95602
(www.PublishingSyndicate.com)

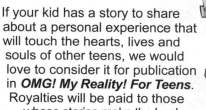

# We Need Stories!

**Not Your Mother's Book...**

On Dating

65 stories about dates that went ... and dates that didn't!

Edited by Dahlynn McKowen, Ken McKowen and Laurel McHa...

**Not Your Mother's Book...**

On Dieting

WTF

...5 funny stories to lighten your load

Edited by Dahlynn McKowen, Ken McKowen and Terri Spilman

**Not Your Mother's Book...**

On Being a Grandparent

65 stories written by experts at spoiling

Edited by Dahlynn McKowen, Ken McKowen and Pat Nelson

**Not Your Mother's Book...**

On Military Life

65 stories from the members and families of our nation's Armed Forces

Edited by Dahlynn McKowen, Ken McKowen and Nelson O. Ottenhausen

**Not Your Mother's Book...**

On Pets

65 pet-approved tales written by their humans

Edited by Dahlynn McKowen, Ken McKowen and Kathleene Baker

Submission guidelines at www.PublishingSyndicate.com

# We Need Stories!

**Not Your Mother's Book...**
**On Menopause**

65 stories about that freakin' change of life
Edited by Dahlynn McKowen,
Ken McKowen and Stacey Hatton

**Not Your Mother's Book...**
**On Embarrassing Moments**

65 hilarious stories about
life's most awkward moments
Edited by Dahlynn McKowen,
Ken McKowen and Pamela Frost

**...Your ...her's Book...**
**On Working for a Living**

65 stories by
working stiffs
Edited by Dahlynn McKowen,
Ken McKowen and Pat Nelson

**Not Your Mother's Boo...**
**On Senior Moments**

65 hilarious stories about aging gracefully
Edited by Dahlynn McKowen
and Ken McKowen

**Not Your Mother's Book...**
**On Sharing Secrets**

65 stories, many told for the very first time
Edited by Dahlynn McKowen,
Ken McKowen and Terri Elders

**Submission guidelines at www.PublishingSyndicate.com**

297